Beautiful Homemaking

Beautiful

Homemaking

By
CHARLENE JOHNSON

Illustrations and
Foreword by
RAYMOND W. JOHNSON

AUGUSTANA PRESS
ROCK ISLAND, ILLINOIS

BEAUTIFUL HOMEMAKING

Second Printing

⟦ PRINTED IN U·S·A ⟧

AUGUSTANA BOOK CONCERN
Printers and Binders
ROCK ISLAND, ILLINOIS
1962

Foreword

TO KNOW the author of this book, my wife Charlene, is to know the radiance of her life, expressed
in the pages of her book, *Beautiful Homemaking*. To
read it is to hear her speak. It is like tuning in on the
radio and turning it off without losing the thrilling
content of its refreshing style and concise message.

The feminine readers of the manuscript for this delightful little book have enthusiastically confirmed the
fact that the author has sensed correctly and met imag-
inatively the spiritual, mental, and physical needs which
are felt by a large portion of modern women. The book
is written in a sparkling conversational tone. One lady
remarked after reading the manuscript: "I felt as if
I were in the midst of an exciting conversation. I found
myself offering aloud notes of approval."

As the warmth of the author's Christian testimony
permeates much of the book, the reader is left with a
thrilling directive: Christ can and should be the very
center of every woman's "beautiful homemaking."

RAYMOND W. JOHNSON

Acknowledgment

THE AUTHOR and sources of the poems have been given wherever it has been possible to do so. This has also been the case with the prose quotations. Should there be any question regarding the use of any poem or quotation without adequate permission, regret is hereby expressed for such unintentional error. Upon notification of such oversight, proper acknowledgment will be made in future editions of this book. The poems, "Life, Twentieth Century" and "Voices from God," are by Victor E. Beck, and are used by permission.

CHARLENE JOHNSON

To Beryl

whose friendship, encouragement,

and understanding have

meant so very much

to me.

Table of Contents

The Home Beautiful

Where there is
Faith
there is Love
Where there is
Love
there is Peace
Where there is
Peace
there is God
Where there is
God
there is no Need

AUTHOR UNKNOWN

CHAPTER ONE

Introduction

THIS is perhaps the most unusual "introduction" ever written to a book; but before you turn another page I want to introduce you to my dearest Friend.

My Friend walks daily with me; He comforts and strengthens me when I need it; He gives me such happiness. I can't even tell you how tall He is, or the color of His hair or eyes. I can't tell you the house He lived in, or His favorite foods. I do know that many library shelves are filled with books written about Him. His Book is the world's best seller. Thousands of buildings have been erected to Him; artists love to paint pictures of Him; composers have written the world's greatest music in dedication to Him.

The lilting song of the bird reminds me of Him; a rushing mountain stream speaks of Him. I think of Him as I stand in awe at the wonder of a starry sky. The snow-capped mountains speak of His majesty; the morning dew on the rosebud speaks of His beauty and artistry. No friend has ever been so true. He has unlimited understanding, tender sympathy, and deep compassion for all. No one has ever loved as He has. No one has ever given himself as He has.

I want to introduce you to my Friend, so that *you* may know Him as *your* Friend too. I must present Him to you because of all He has done for me. Within my soul I had a deep hunger to know God. True, I had always believed there was a God. I had attended church occasionally, and even gone through religious training; but I wasn't satisfied. I needed so much more.

And then it was that I met my Friend—personally. I was introduced to Him by the "glow" of the lives of some of His friends. I knew they had found what I was searching for. And so, in the darkness of the night, I knelt by a bed and asked my Friend to walk with me for evermore. In spite of myself, He loved me, He forgave my sins, and He welcomed my friendship. It was like walking out of the depths of night into the glorious dawn of a new day. My hunger was satisfied! My needs were met! All the angels of heaven rejoiced because I, a sinner, had found the Savior, the Lord Jesus Christ.

CHARLENE JOHNSON

"Behold, I am with you and will keep you wherever you go."

Genesis 28:15

CHAPTER TWO

Have a Cup of Coffee, Mother?

DEAR Mothers! Do sit down and relax! That's right, put your feet up on the footstool, and sip your coffee while we chat. In fact, let's make a date for the next few days to have a morning coffee party together— a chapter of this book every morning with your cup of coffee. If *Beautiful Homemaking* gives you a little more sunshine in your life, a little more spring in your step, a little more determination to be the most beautiful wife and mother you can possibly be, inwardly and outwardly, and—most important of all—if this book

3

brings you just a step closer to our wonderful Lord of light, life, and joy—Jesus Christ—the Savior, then the purpose of *Beautiful Homemaking* will have been accomplished.

Some people are puzzled over my way of thinking. They wonder how beauty and loveliness can possibly be associated with Christianity. They feel that there is a huge gulf between the two. I don't! I believe with all my heart that our Savior wants each one of us to be at her best in every way: the way we think and feel and look. He wants us to be at our best from the tops of our heads to the bottoms of our feet, outwardly and inwardly. For *true beauty is spiritual*; it radiates from within, and is revealed on the outside.

We all have met, I am sure, women who are strikingly attractive, who know just how to style their hair, apply their make-up, and dress in good taste; who are well groomed; whose posture is perfect; who are graceful, yet for whom beauty is nothing but a hard, cold, vain shell. This is not beauty! This is a cheap imita-

4

tion. Look for the heavenly beauty and joy that is shining from a heart filled with love for our mighty God and for *all* of His children—yes, *His children* of *all* colors and races and creeds, and from *all* walks of life. This is true beauty! It can be seen.

MIRRORED PRAYER

Do you know, my fellow Christians,
All the time and every place
Men are looking for the image of
The Master in your face?
And the image you're reflecting
Is distorted or is fair
Just according to the measure
Of the time you spend in prayer.

Youth's Favorite Poems, III, 29

It hurts me when I see people looking at professing Christians and saying, "Tch tch, isn't it too bad?" when what they should be saying is, "That person's got something! I *need* what that person has!" All around us people are crying for that "something." Billions of aspirins are being sold yearly, the popularity of tranquilizers is rapidly increasing, psychiatrists' couches are full, the "happiness" books sell by the millions. Why? Because people are searching . . . searching . . . searching. For what? For the answer that lies *only* in the Christian faith. If Christians everywhere were truly "glowing" for their Lord, the world would see that we have the answer, and would come into our churches eagerly to find it.

5

Over the years Christian people have sometimes been stereotyped: long faces, *always* dark clothes, and drab personalities to boot. This is utter nonsense! Let's take color for example. All a person has to do is to look at God's breath-takingly beautiful world—the colorful hues of autumn, the brilliant flowers of springtime, the sunrises, the sunsets, and a rainbow, to see how much God himself must love color and beauty, for He is the creator of it!

And those long, sad faces—shame on us! How can a true child of God wear one? Why, if anyone has the right to love life and radiate happiness and joy and beauty and confidence, it is the one who knows the Lord Jesus Christ as his personal Savior and Friend. This is living! Our Lord said, "I came that they may have life, and have it abundantly" (John 10:10).

Listen to the Bible!

Rejoice in the Lord always; again I will say, Rejoice (Philippians 4:4).

Look to him, and be radiant (Psalm 34:5).

Happy is the man who listens to me, watching daily at my gates, waiting beside my doors (Proverbs 8:34).

"O taste and see that the Lord is good! Happy is the man who takes refuge in him! (Psalm 34:8).

"Hallelujah! For the Lord our God the Almighty reigns. Let us rejoice and exult and give him the glory" (Revelation 19:6, 7).

Think of the confidence and trust He has put in us; He has said, "Let your light so shine before men, that they may see your good works and give glory to your Father who is in heaven"; and, "You are the light of the world." Incredible! Unworthy and sinful though we are, He looks confidently to us to be the light of the world. How great our responsibility! We cannot fail Him, the Lord of light, the one who has given us spiritual light. Perhaps I can express it more clearly by comparing spiritual light and blindness with the physical. Let us suppose that a woman has been blind since birth. The skilled hands of the surgeon have performed a miraculous operation on her eyes, so that she is now able to see. Can you imagine her joy, her radiant happiness, when for the first time she sees the light? How much greater should our joy be when our spiritual blindness is replaced by spiritual light and we see for the first time the glory of our Lord! Let God's light radiate through you.

Yes, mothers, God's light should be glowing through us even in the humblest duties in the home. As housewives perhaps our greatest need is for a "housekeeping" Christianity, the kind that should be in use while we wash, iron, scrub, and wax. Our lives are routine in many ways; it seems as though our work is never finished. Some days are trying, nerves become frayed, and even our enthusiasm dims at times. That is why we must have a "housekeeping" Christianity.

"If we would enjoy His guidance in the big things of life we must practice following Him in the small, everyday decisions, and then we will not find it difficult to hear His voice saying, 'This is the way, walk ye in it.'" AUTHOR UNKNOWN

Christ intends us to live our religion in terms of our everyday life. The secret is to see God in all that we do. Take, for example, the job of getting the children off to school and hubby off to work in the morning. Instead of rushing everyone off as fast as you can, decide that your most important duty of the morning is to do everything possible to see that your family is in a relaxed, happy frame of mind when they leave their home, so that they will all start the day joyfully because of you, dear mother.

Someone has said, "Be pleasant until 10 o'clock in the morning, and the rest of the day will take care of itself."

Or, let's take this business of scrubbing and cleaning. Why not consider it symbolic of the clean and orderly life of God's children? This will give your job new importance. Consider every bit of work you do in your home an expression of your love for your family.

Dr. Reuben Youngdahl in his book, *Live Today*, entitles one of his meditations, "Walking in God's Smile." What a beautiful thought! Let's carry that thought with us *every* day of our lives.

This joy, this happiness, this enthusiasm which I am talking about is not something light or superficial; it is deep and profound. The happiest people I know are the ones who have learned to be happy at what they are, at where they are, and in what they are doing. The Apostle Paul put it this way, "I have learned, in whatever state I am, to be content."

MY KITCHEN PRAYER

Bless my pretty kitchen, Lord,
And light it with Thy love;
Help me plan and cook my meals
From Thy heavenly home above.
Bless our meals with Thy presence
And warm them with Thy grace;
Watch over me as I do my work,
Washing pots and pans and plates.
The service I am trying to do
Is to make my family content
So bless my eager efforts, Lord
And make them heaven sent.

AUTHOR UNKNOWN

9

Yes, the prayer offered with hands that are cooking, scrubbing, ironing, or dressing little ones is given the same loving attention as the prayers offered with folded hands.

JUST TO BE THERE

Prayer is so simple;
It is like quietly opening a door
And stepping into the very presence of God.
There in the stillness
To hear His voice;
Perhaps to petition
Or only to listen;
It matters not.
Just to be there
In His presence
Is prayer.

Youth's Favorite Poems, III, 7

He is with us every moment of every hour of every day to encourage, to comfort, to forgive, and to give great joy. We are walking toward the sun! May God help us all to "glow" as we walk, to be truly "beautiful" in the richest and fullest sense of the word.

With this guiding spirit, mothers, let's go through this book together. We'll talk about homemaking, and how it can be beautiful, and how you can be your most beautiful self. We'll talk about husbands, and even a little *to* husbands (see "Letter to Daddy," chapter 5), about how to care for our wonderful children, and even have a story for them; about how to make our home our paradise (not only housekeeping tips, but also decorating ideas). Hospitality is so important, and it's easy to be hospitable with a little basic know-how that will help us to be relaxed and efficient hostesses. I think that we mothers must seriously ask ourselves the question, "How big is our world?" and, of course, our last consideration, and the most important one, must be our personal relationship with God; the last chapter is entitled, "Your God and You."

So, on we go! But first, do have another cup of coffee.

A BEAUTIFUL EPITAPH:

She kept her tears to herself,
But shared her happiness

God is a God of laughter, as well as of prayer . . . a
    God of singing,
as well as of tears.
God is at home in the play of His children
He loves to hear us laugh.

We do not honor God by our long faces . . . our austerity.
God wants us to be good—not "goody-goody."
There is quite a distinction.

We must try to make the distinction between worship
    and work
    and play
less sharp . . .

11

If God is not in your typewriter as well as your hymn-
    book,
  there is something wrong with your religion.
If your God does not enter your kitchen
  there is something the matter with your kitchen.
If you can't take God into your recreation
  there is something wrong with the way you play.
If God, for you, does not smile,
  there is something wrong with your idea of God.

From Dr. Peter Marshall's sermon entitled, "Do Whatever He Tells You." In
A Man Called Peter. Used by permission
of McGraw-Hill Book Company, Inc.

CHAPTER THREE

Beautiful
Homemaking

NOW, how can homemaking possibly be beautiful? Why, even that word "housewife" carries with it a drab, humdrum quality, doesn't it? But—"tain't necessarily so!" The housewife's profession is just about the most challenging in the world—and the most rewarding. Not only is she a wife, and perhaps a mother, but also a housekeeper, a cook, an accountant, a nurse, a teacher, a psychologist, a diplomat, a social secretary, a friend, and a sweetheart; and her most important job is to be the very center of love and sunshine in the home. Her highest motivation is love. It's extremely important that the housewife make the most of every one of her God-given abilities and talents, so that her life, her family, her home, her neighbors, her world, and her faith might all revolve in beautiful harmony.

A housewife's rewards are the greatest in the world. Who can measure the value of a husband's loving embrace and the words, "Darling, you're wonderful!" or the sweet kiss of your child and his priceless words, "I love you, Mommy!"? Then you are a *millionaire!*

Beautiful homemaking! Let's begin by talking about mother herself. Only housewives can truly appreciate one another's concerns, problems, worries, and joys. I wish I could express to you all that is within my heart. It is difficult for anyone who endeavors to write to make it clear to her readers that she is not putting herself on a soap box and talking "down" to others. God knows that the only finger I am pointing is directly at myself. I am writing about all of these things because *I* need to be reminded of them. Somehow I feel that perhaps many of my needs and weaknesses and problems are yours, too. *Together* let us search and find and grow.

Our schedule *is* routine! Breakfast to get in the morning, children to dress, hubby to send off to work, dishes to do, dusting, vacuuming, washing, ironing, mending, polishing, cooking—how can we add beauty, sugar, and spice to the regularity of our daily routine? It begins with *you!*

If your life is bubbling with Christian happiness, radiance, and enthusiasm, it will blossom out into all of your world. The Bible tells us, that "a cheerful heart is a good medicine." Joy will bring health and vitality

14

to every part of your being. The happiness of your life depends upon your thoughts. How does your *thinking* run—uphill or downhill?

> *The pleasantest things in the world are pleasant thoughts, and the great art in life is to have as many of them as possible.*
>
> C. N. BOREE

As you go about your housework, count your blessings. Work in a sunbath of cheer. Shut out thoughts that hurt. Turn everything so that you see its brightest side. When worry comes, think of something else, something bright and beautiful. God's Word puts it this way: "Whatever is true, whatever is honorable, whatever is just, whatever is pure, whatever is lovely, whatever is gracious, . . . think about these things."

> *Think how lucky you are*
> *and be happy . . .*
> *You have friends who are*
> *loving and true;*
> *You have blessings galore*
> *all around you . . .*
> *You have health and you've*
> *something to do!*
> *Think how lucky you are*
> *and be thankful*
> *To the One who sent all*
> *these your way . . .*
> *It's a wonderful world*
> *that you live in*

15

So . . . just live and be
happy today!

Keep in mind that every minute you are sad you lose sixty seconds of happiness. Someone once said: "There are souls in this world which have the gift of finding joy everywhere and of leaving it behind them wherever they go." Be numbered among them! Some are downhearted because there are thorns among the roses; others are thrilled because there are roses among the thorns. Which kind are you?

Pity the millions who believe that happiness consists in having and getting and being served by others. How lucky are those who have learned that happiness is to be had through giving and serving others. William Wordsworth wrote, "The best portion of a good person's life; his little nameless, unremembered acts of kindness and love." To be of use in the world is the only way to be happy.

LIVE AS YOU PRAY

I knelt to pray when day was done,
And prayed, "O Lord, bless every one;
Lift from each saddened heart the pain,
And let the sick be well again."

And then I woke another day
And carelessly went on my way.
The whole day long I did not try
To wipe a tear from any eye;

16

I did not try to share the load
  Of any brother on my road;
I did not even go to see
  The sick man just next door to me.

Yet once again when day was done
  I prayed, "O Lord, bless every one."
But as I prayed, into my ear
  There came a voice that whispered clear:

"Pause, hypocrite, before you pray,
  Whom have you tried to bless today?
God's sweetest blessings always go
  By hands that serve Him here below."

And then I hid my face, and cried,
  "Forgive me, God, for I have lied;
Let me but see another day
  And I will live the way I pray."

Youth's Favorite Poems, II, 6

The glory of life is to love,
  not to be loved;
to give, not to get;
to serve, not to be served.

HUGH BLACK

When the blues start to get hold of me, I often think of the personal experience of a California housewife

which I read about not long ago. The newspaper head-
lines were grim, the weather cloudy, the regularity of
life exasperating. She asked herself, "What can I, one
woman, do to make life a little brighter?" "I must do
something, no matter how small, to make this world a
better place." Her heart told her, "*Love* is the answer."
Her head said, "Before you can make the world brighter,
you must clean house within yourself. Sweep out everything foreign to love." But one cannot do this alone.
This is the time to reach out to the Hand of Love for
support. *God is love.* Without Him, there is no gen-
uine love; for His is the only perfect love. She asked,
and He answered. She learned to love the Lord of lords,
and His great love was now glowing through her. She
found *she* had to help. She had to shake out the dust
of envy, malice, and greed, and discovered that we are
not what we *think* we are, but that what we *think,* we
are!

She started with her home, making life a little better
for those she lived with. She let love tell her what to
do. Up early the next morning, she told her sleepy
hubby, "Let me bring you some coffee in bed, dear."
He was shocked, astonished, but happy. She got the
coffee, kissed him, and told him softly, "I love you."
She'd never said it so boldly. She asked him what he
wanted for breakfast and could see the pleasure shining in his eyes, for this had made him feel important.

She woke up her son and called him "darling." Half
blushing, he came out of his room tugging at his blue
jeans and asked, "Did you call me darling, Mom?" His
luminous little face couldn't hide the fact that he *did*
like it. They'd never been a demonstrative family—

but why not? Why not let the people we love know it? We are so desperately afraid of sentiment. We say "Goodbye" when we mean, "God be with you; I'll be so lonesome for you." When someone pays us a compliment, we say, "Thanks" instead of "How kind you are; you've made me feel so good." And the list could go on and on. What a funny world! God help us all to be softer, kinder, warmer, and more loving in all that we say and do! This is spiritual strength, not weakness.

Thus the life of the entire family was changed. They thought of little ways to make each other happy, to make each other smile. They learned to praise one another, and their home became "a little bit of heaven."

Let me be a little kinder,
Let me be a little blinder
To the faults of those about me;
Let me praise a little more.

Let me be, when I am weary,
Just a little bit more cheery;
Let me serve a little better
Those whom I am striving for.

Let me be a little meeker
With the other who is weaker;
Let me think more of my neighbor
And a little less of me.

Youth's Favorite Poems, I, 14

Next, she moved out into her neighborhood. She brought a cake to an eighty-four-year-old neighbor for whom she had not previously had much time. The dear little lady was thrilled to know that someone had thought of her; she asked shyly, "Do you mind if I give you a little kiss?" With lips as soft as rose petals she kissed the housewife on the cheek. A week later the old woman passed through the veil into the other life with a smile on her face, and the housewife never forgot the rose petal kiss. Our housewifes' coffee parties now included many older neighbors, many lonely ones as well as her closer friends. Yes, the world is full of lonely people of all ages. They should be invited to a party! They so need to feel important, to know that someone cares. No love, no friendship, no kindness, is ever wasted.

The keys to a beautiful personality are just the things we have been talking about: love and kindness. Everyone wants to be liked by others. What are the char-

acteristics of a "likable" person? Well, a likable person sparkles! She is warm. You know, "warmth" is something you can feel, something you respond to. It works like a magnet. Imagine yourself walking down the street and passing an old acquaintance. If that person smiles and greets you with warmth and enthusiasm, you feel good all over, right? If, on the other hand, she gives you a cool greeting, something inside of you freezes up. Be genuinely warm! "He who would have friends must show himself friendly."

The likable person talks enthusiastically, but about you and your interests mainly. Her conversation is rarely centered around the famous three: me, myself, and I. She's an interesting person because she's well read. She knows what's going on in the world. She reads *good* books, and *inspiring* magazine articles. What the mind feeds on helps to determine what the person will be. The likable person is a good listener; she looks people in the eye, and is interested in what they are saying. She doesn't interrupt and tries never to be disinterested when another is talking. That would be rude. She's kind in what she says and does and thinks. What is it the wise old owl once said? "If you can't say something nice, don't say anything at all."

Do you really want to learn to enjoy others? Then learn to love them for what they are, for what they can become. We're all so full of faults. We stumble and fall so often. Our Lord was the only one who ever walked this earth who did not sin. Look for the good in all people; sincerely, honestly love people, and many of them will love you in return. Charles Dickens once rephrased the golden rule to read this way, "Try to do

21

to others as you would have them do to you, and don't be disappointed if they fail sometimes." Love is contagious.

Friendship is such a rich treasure; you will gain and grow a little with each new friendship. The only sure way to destroy an enemy is to make him your friend. A true friend sees the best in us, and for that reason calls forth the very best that is in us. In many ways we are what we are expected to be. It has been said that a friend is a bank of credit on which we can draw supplies of confidence, counsel, sympathy, help, and love. Be a true friend, for the hinges of true friendship *never* grow rusty. Two persons will not be friends long, if they cannot forgive one another's failures. It is pleasant to have people love you even when they don't know you; but of far more value is the love of a friend who knows you and still loves you.

To me, this is the greatest wonder of Christianity: to think that He knows us through and through, and that He yet loves us!

Homemaking can be beautiful, but only when every part of *you,* dear mother, is beautiful.

The brave, blind, dauntless Helen Keller once said: "Join the great company of those who make the barren places of life fruitful with kindness. Carry a vision of heaven in your hearts, and you shall make your home, the world, correspond to that vision. Your success and happiness lie in you. The great, enduring realities are love and service. Joy is the holy fire that keeps our purpose warm and our intelligence aglow. Resolve to keep happy and your joy and you shall form an invincible host against difficulty."

CHAPTER FOUR

Beautiful You

Lord, make me an instrument of Thy peace.
Where there is hate, may I bring love;
Where offense, may I bring pardon;
May I bring union in place of discord;
Truth, replacing error;
Faith, where once there was doubt;
Hope for despair
Light, where was darkness;
Joy, to replace sadness.
Make me not to so crave to be loved as to love.
Help me to learn that in giving I may receive;
In forgetting self, I may find life eternal.

ST. FRANCIS OF ASSISI

HAVE you ever looked at a "before" and "after" picture of a woman, and wished that someone would just take you under her wing and show you how to be your most attractive self? Well, mother, that's just the purpose of this chapter. Not every woman can be breath-takingly beautiful, but *every* woman can be attractive outwardly and beautiful inwardly.

We must never make the mistake of thinking that beauty alone is sufficient. Only in nature or in inanimate objects, such as statues or paintings, does beauty alone suffice. To understand the importance of physical beauty in its proper perspective and place is indeed a mark of an intelligent woman. I think we all know that when we look our best, we feel our best and act our best. It adds so much to our confidence and poise. It is when we *exaggerate* the importance of physical beauty that we stand on shaky ground. The eternal qualities of the mind, heart, and soul are the qualities that truly count in the sight of God and man.

A famous marriage counselor illustrated this point vividly when he told the true story of one of his counselees. Mrs. X, a woman separated from her husband, had come to the counselor for advice on another marriage which she was considering. Mrs. X was an extremely beautiful woman, expensively dressed, and perfectly groomed. All her life she'd had everything given to her on a silver platter. This was the reason behind the failure of her first marriage. She had demanded, and received, a fabulous home, cars, clothes, and furniture which her husband simply could not afford. She wanted this and she wanted that, and consistently demanded that she have these things. She did not realize

24

that empty lives are empty still, though filled with "things." Her husband, downhearted and nearly bankrupt, could not take it any longer, and they had separated.

The counselor listened intently to Mrs. X's side of the story, and then he said to her: "I'd like you to hear something." Then he called in the elderly office janitress. He said to the janitress, "Will you please tell Mrs. X how you found happiness in life?" And the dear janitress began her story.

"Well, my husband died of pneumonia, and three months later my only son was killed in an accident. I had nobody or nothing; I walked in a daze; I couldn't sleep; I didn't feel like eating; I never smiled at anyone or anything. I'd even thought of doing away with myself.

"One night a scrawny kitten followed me home from work. Somehow, I felt sorry for that kitten; it was cold outside, and I decided to let the kitten in, and I gave it some milk. It purred and rubbed against my leg, and for the first time in months I smiled. Then I stopped to think: If helping a little kitten could make me smile, maybe doing something for somebody else would make me happy. So the next day I baked some

25

goodies and took them to a neighbor who was sick in bed. Every day I tried to do something nice for some one else, because it made me so happy to see them happy. I guess a person can't be very happy, unless he's thinking of how much he can help others instead of how much he can get. I don't know of anybody who sleeps and eats better than I do. I've found happiness."

When the janitress had finished her story the counselor noticed that tears were trickling down Mrs. X's cheeks. "You don't need to say anything," Mrs. X said softly, "I'm going to make a 'human being' out of this useless, silly doll that I've always been." She had seen how hollow physical beauty and things alone can be.

> It's good to have money and the things
>   money can buy—
> but, it's good too, to check up once in
>   a while and make sure that you haven't
> lost the things money can't buy.

AUTHOR UNKNOWN

Now that we understand and appreciate the importance of inward and outward beauty, we're ready to talk about *you* and how you can look your prettiest. Watch your husband glow like a bridegroom, and notice how proud your children will be of you when you make those "extra efforts" to look your best. Let your goal be "to look my best from head to toe."

POSTURE

This is the number one figure fault of women everywhere. Slouch in front of a mirror, and then stand up straight. See what a tremendous change takes place in your appearance just by holding yourself erectly? Much can be told about a woman's personality just by the way she carries herself. If she is relaxed, poised, and self-confident, it can usually be seen in her good posture. Here is the "recipe" for good posture;

- Tummy pulled *way in!*

- Buttock tucked *way under!*

- Chest held high—as if you were being pulled upward by two magic strings.

- Chin up.

- Shoulders relaxed.

Try it—now. If it hurts, it's because you're not standing that way all the time. You'll feel better and healthier, if you stand correctly. Think tall! Walk tall! Stand tall! Feel tall! Sit tall!

WALKING

- One foot in front of the other as if following a line.
- Toes "ever so slightly" out.
- Hips move smoothly—no swaying from side to side.
- No heel clicking, please.
- Arms relaxed.
- Posture perfect.
- No bouncing. *Smoothness* is the key word for correct walking. Imagine that you are "gliding" along.

SITTING

Let the back of your legs touch the front of the chair. Sit down on the edge of the chair, keeping your back straight, and slide back. To get up, slide forward to the edge of the chair, and get up with your back straight. While sitting, keep your ankles and knees together, whether your legs are crossed or not. Practice, practice, practice!

DIET

Almost every woman has some kind of weight problem. Either she is too fat or too thin, or else the pounds need to be redistributed. And you can push the pounds around! Let's tackle these problems one by one.

OVERWEIGHT

This, of course, is the most common problem. We simply eat too well. This is our only alternative: we must change our eating habits permanently. Did you know that the woman who loses 75 to 100 pounds is much more likely to keep those pounds off than is the woman who lost 10? Do you know why? Because a woman who has lost a large amount of weight has learned to eat *differently*. Two to three months of correct eating will have changed your eating habits. Forget those two-week crash diets. Learn to eat and enjoy the right foods in the right quantities. If you are accustomed to eating a lot, your tummy has stretched and, consequently, you need lots of food to fill it. This is the reason that many of these appetite-appeasing pills are helpful to women with big appetites. But once you have accustomed yourself to eating smaller amounts, your tummy will shrink, and you will not need as much food to keep you satisfied.

29

Let's face it! We all know very well which foods are low in calorie content and which are high. If you are not sure, or want more information, pick up a twenty-five cent calorie counter at your corner drug store. But, believe me, it *is* the sweet rolls, the rich desserts, the starchy food and greasy foods that are responsible for those excess pounds. Learn really to love salads, vegetables, juices, lots of meats, eggs, skim milk, etc. Here is an acceptable daily diet for an average housewife:

- I pint milk
- 4 servings vegetable (include raw, leafy vegetables)
- 1 serving meat, fish, or poultry
- 1 egg
- 2 servings fruit (1 citrus)
- 1 serving cereal or enriched bread
- 1 pat butter
- Some sweets (1 tsp sugar = 16 calories)

If we're honest with ourselves, we'll face the fact that we as housewives have two main diet hindrances:

1. We're home most of the time, and "snacking" is just too easy.
2. We have to cook to please our families, and we haven't the will power to refrain from eating some of these "yummy" delicacies that we put on the table.

The answers?

1. Will power! Backbone! Common sense! If you ate only at mealtime, and drank only a glass of juice, skim milk, or coffee mid morning, mid afternoon, and at bedtime, do you think you'd be struggling with those ten or fifteen extra pounds? Be honest now, do you? Discipline yourself to this kind of eating schedule. Paste a picture of a very fat woman inside your refrigerator and cupboard doors—as a reminder when you are tempted to nibble. When you do your grocery shopping, don't buy those high-calorie foods that you are so tempted to snack on. Juice, coffee, rusks, hard-boiled eggs, fruit—these must be your snack foods. If you cheat, you're cheating no one but yourself. It's up to you, mother. Do you really want to wear that size 12 dress again? Do you honestly want to look your best? Then you must sacrifice a little! Chances are your neighbors would love a suggestion that *just* coffee be served at morning coffee parties. Remember— it's up to *you!!*

2. Here's a little trick for you to try. There are probably some desserts and rolls that your husband likes very well that you are not quite as fond of. Serve these. In my own case, I know that if chocolate is around, I can't resist it. My husband isn't very fond of chocolate, so I fix and buy other goodies for him and our children, and I find that the temptation to indulge isn't nearly as great. The only time I fix rich, whipped creamy desserts is when company is coming. I think a family is better off in general when the members eat less of the sweets and starches and more fruits, vegeta-

31

bles, and high protein foods. Your whole family will feel better if you eat better.

Let's talk for a few moments about will power. Without discipline, dieters can't do the job. You must not be wishy-washy.

Did you know that medical studies have shown that eighty per cent or more of all dieters, whether they want to lose four pounds or forty, fail to take it off and keep it off? Why? Not because their intentions were not good, but because they lacked stick-to-itiveness.

Generally speaking, people who take off weight and keep it off have several personality traits in common: they are usually intelligent, mature, neat, and concerned about others. So, keep your goal in mind, ask your family to encourage you, and remember that you *will* have to sacrifice. But remember also that the rewards will be worth every sacrifice. Don't become discouraged if the pounds don't roll off as fast as you'd like. We all lose weight at different rates of speed—some slowly, others quickly; others slow at first, and then fast; and still others fast, and then slow. But don't give up! You *can* do it;—keep telling yourself that!

UNDERWEIGHT

Many underweights are quick, high-tensioned people. To begin with, they must learn to relax—at mealtime, after mealtime, and as they work. They must eat the correct foods, but they should add all the extras: lots of butter and cream sauces, etc. A bedtime snack is a must for them.

WEIGHT IN THE WRONG PLACES: EXERCISE

No matter what your category is, exercise is a *must* for that tingling feeling of good health, and for that lovely and well-proportioned figure. Five to ten minutes of regular exercise *every day* are far more beneficial than an hour of exercise once a week. In my book, *Altogether Lovely,* I have listed and explained exercises for all parts of the body. Again we need self-discipline. I know that your mornings are rushed, and you are tired in the evenings; but do set a definite time every day for your exercising. Perhaps the best time will be during the children's nap time. Take time every day for physical exercises. But keep in mind how much more important it is that you take time for spiritual exercise every day. Bible reading, prayer, and meditation are a spiritual exercise. Without this daily spiritual exercise we can never remain spiritually healthy. Punctuate your day with prayer. Spurgeon once said, "You need a daily supply. Day by day you must seek help from above. It is a very sweet assurance that a daily portion is provided for *you."*

PREGNANCY

Pregnancy can be a beautiful experience, or an uncomfortable one; you can enjoy your pregnancy, or you can endure it. There are so many helpful little ideas to list.

Remember that you do not have to eat for two. Eat all of the essential food basics we have talked about—lots of skim milk (hi-vitamin) and dairy products, and stay away from starches and sweets. I'm going to tell you about my experience, because I think you'll probably learn a lesson from it. When I was pregnant for the first time I gained thirty-seven pounds. I didn't feast all the time either. I just ate well-rounded meals (and became well rounded, I might add). The doctor who took care of me during my second pregnancy kept me very weight conscious; he gave me pills to appease my appetite, and told me which foods to stay away from. I'll always be grateful to him. I only gained twelve pounds during my second pregnancy, and felt better than I'd ever felt in my life. Incidentally, my first baby weighed 7 pounds 6 ounces, my second weighed 7 pounds 5 ounces—two healthy, happy boys. You do *not* have to eat for two.

Here is one of the best little tidbits of advice a pregnant woman will ever hear: *Never, never* stick your tummy out. Sound impossible? Even when you are nine months along, pretend that you can pull your tummy in, and try to keep full control of your tummy muscles. Posture perfect? Good! If you keep control of your tummy muscles, you'll find it a simple matter to spring back into shape after the baby arrives. The reason many women never have flat tummies after they have children is because they have lost control of their stomach muscles and they are not willing to exercise to build up that muscle control again. Start exercising regularly as soon as you have your doctor's permission. I started breathing exercises while I was still in the hospital. One of the happiest moments I had was being able to wear a sheath dress home from the hospital after my second child was born. *Exercise! Exercise!* Sit-ups are excellent, so is the exercise which has you lying on the floor on your back, arms and legs spread out. Bring the right leg up to touch the left hand and vise versa. Or, here's another: lie on the floor, lift both legs about five inches off the floor, knees straight, and do the scissors with your feet. Every day! You'll never be sorry for making those extra efforts to keep your figure.

If there ever was a time to make every effort to look lovely, this is it. Maternity clothes are simple to sew, and the styles are so sharp and pretty now that they are fun to wear. Pick the prettiest, gayest colors. Put special emphasis on your hair-do, complexion, and accessories, and your personal grooming. Do wear gloves, pretty shoes, and tasteful jewelry when you go out.

Don't baby yourself—not very much, anyway. Enjoy your pregnancy (give or take a few weeks for morning sickness). Remember that millions of women are going through this same wonderful experience. Keep active. Don't sit around and think about yourself. Think about that precious little bundle that soon will be placed in your tender arms by our heavenly Father. Do get enough rest and fresh air. Follow your doctor's advice. Read! Keep your minds alive and alert. Together with your husband plan baby's room, baby's layette, share ideas on caring for the baby and, of course, spend lots of time deciding on a name (a boy's name and a girl's name). Don't set your hearts on one sex or the other. You and husband will both love either a boy or girl equally well, because your child is the blessed fruit of your love, your marriage; your baby is the God-given fulfillment of your most deeply felt hopes and aspirations.

And with this great privilege comes responsibility. Yes, the great blessing that comes from feeling a tiny hand grasping your finger in love and trust, the blessing we receive from watching our baby's eyes laughing into ours, the blessing we know from directing our child's mind and body as the child grows into the most beautiful of all creations: a godly man or woman—yes, these blessings carry with them great responsibility. Shoulder it well, dear mother.

COMPLEXION CARE

Oh, how we all long to have and to keep young, glowing complexions! Here are a few wonderful ideas for accomplishing this:

36

"Laughter keeps the face and heart young."—Anon.

Dicken's recipe for keeping young and lovely, "Cheerfulness and content are great beautifiers and are famous preservers of youthful looks."

Our inner life is revealed on our faces. If the beauty of Christ is within us, it can be seen on our face.

It is important, too, that we learn how to care for our complexions, how to keep them fresh and glowing. Your own good health is extremely important. I believe in vitamin capsules as well as a nutritious diet, such as suggested earlier. Exercise, eight hours of sleep nightly, and fresh air are all important. Try this: Cleanse your face and neck thoroughly, put on only a little lipstick, and go for a brisk walk outdoors. Let God's fresh air penetrate your skin. Bundle up the children, and take them with you. You know, I often think that perhaps we are getting too soft. We do need more fresh air and outdoor activity. How does that sound to you? Do give it a try. It may give you a real lift.

In facial cleansing use the five dot method when applying any cream or lotion or liquid make-up. Fingers move from the center of the forehead to the sides, and from the center of the chin to the sides and up to the cheeks.

1. Use a good liquid cleansing cream on your face at least twice a day.

2. Tissue off cream, and follow with astringent applied with a puff of cotton.

3. What you do to your face, do to your neck also. Mmmmmmm! Now, don't you feel freshened up?

MAKE-UP

Make-up is an individual matter. *Never* should make-up look artificial, hard, or unladylike; but up to that point it is *you* who must decide personally on the amount of make-up you wish to use.

Make-up is not essential. Some women look and feel loveliest with no more than just the slightest touch of a light lipstick. We are all different personalities, of different ages, and we have different backgrounds, and live in different situations and localities; but let us be very careful not to be critical of one another in this matter of make-up. Every woman must do what she believes to be right. I am including this section on make-up *only* for the women who are looking for advice on how to use make-up.

The purpose of make-up is simply to bring out your prettiest features and to subdue the features that are not quite so pretty. Let's begin with the eyebrows. Few women know how correctly to pluck their brows. You do *not* change the natural shape of your eyebrows. You simply clean out stray hairs from between the brows and the strays from under your brows. *Never* pluck above the brow. A well-groomed brow will give your entire face a neater and brighter appearance.

Eyebrow pencil. If pencil is used, a light brown pencil is used for blondes and brownettes, and a dark brown pencil for brunettes. The pencil should be very sharp. Carefully sketch—with light, feathery strokes across the tops of your brows and fill in *lightly* any blank areas. Your pencil should not be noticeable; your pencil should look like part of your brow.

Make-up base. Personally, I prefer a light textured liquid base and just a faint whisper of powder on the nose. However, women with oily complexions will be happier with a combination base and powder which comes in a little compact. When buying make-up, test it on your forehead, not on your hand, because your hands and face are not the same shade. The match should be almost perfect. When you apply your base, follow the five point method, blending the base gently onto your neck, too.

Lipstick. I think we can safely say that many women do a very poor job of applying their lipstick. Lipstick is not to be applied in the "general area" of the mouth, but rather it is clearly to define the lips. Try a light lip liner pencil or lip brush; fill in with the lipstick. It does take practice. Remember that a dark mouth is a hard mouth; a light, bright lipstick is always prettier, more natural and feminine looking.

Now for that special occasion! If you wish, try a drop of cream on each eyelid, a bit of mascara on the tips of your lashes, perhaps a few seconds with an eyelash curler, and you're ready for a gala evening.

39

GOOD GROOMING

"She's perfectly groomed," is a compliment every woman would like to hear. And with a little time and effort every woman can be well groomed.

We must begin with the daily bubble bath or shower. You know, mother, the bath can be a close friend, and the answer to many problems.

● It can be a stimulant. Let's suppose that you and your husband are invited out, and you are simply worn to a frazzle. Step into a hot bubble bath; your blood zooms to the skin's surface, and you can't help but feel stimulated.

● It can be a sedative. Yes, the bath can relieve tensions, and relax you when you need it.

● It can be a good location for applying cream to your face, setting your hair, and even filing your nails. The steam is a boon to all of these little tasks, making them even more effective.

● It is the best place to squander scents. Did you know that fragrances spread by steam and water stay with you longer? Smell as lovely as you are.

Yes, let your bath be your oasis!

After your bath, dry yourself in a big, fluffy towel, puff on bath powder or, if your skin tends to be dry, use a smoothing, body lotion.

Of course, you use a deoderant daily, and you shave underarms and legs once a week, and give yourselves a weekly manicure and pedicure. These are musts. Now, time to check your clothes. You are *never* well dressed unless you are perfectly well groomed.

● Are your clothes free of lint, spots, and stains?

● Are they pressed to perfection?

● Are the seams tightly stitched?

● Are your white clothes *really* white?

● Are the cotton blouses "crisp"?

● Are the shoes polished and the heels in good condition?

● Forswear safety pins, twisted belts, loose buttons, and any other wardrobe grooming weaknesses you may have.

Be tidy as a pin! Practice the art of perfect groom ing daily until it becomes a habit with you.

HAIR

You can do just about anything with your hair, with practice and know-how and effort. In order to be lovely, your hair must be healthy. And once again, healthy hair stems from a healthy body.

Hair must be kept clean. Most women find they must wash their hair every five to eight days. Experiment with various shampoos. Lots of lather and lots and lots and lots of rinsing—the secret of successful shampooing. Any soap left in the hair will make the hair dull. Do use a cream rinse on your hair when you've finished your shampoo; it will make your hair sparkle and much easier to manage.

Comb out your wet hair with a large, clean comb; allow it to dry partially; then, using wave set, set your hair on rollers or with smooth pin curls held in place by hair clips which do not crimp your curls as bobby pins do. Follow fashion trends sensibly when it comes to selecting a hair style. Consider the shape of your face, your build (a tiny girl looks overpowered with too much hair, a big girl looks small headed with a tiny hairdo), your personality, your way of life, and the texture of your hair. It's fun to have a hairdo that is somewhat versatile. Consult a highly recommended professional hair stylist for advice and a basic hair shaping.

Brush your hair regularly every day, and you'll be amazed at the results, even in a few weeks' time.

When your hair is dry, brush out the set. Yes, I said brush. Brushing shows off a pretty set. Hairdos should never look "tight." Soft, relaxed, and feminine—this is the secret of a lovely hair style.

WARDROBE

It is not necessary to be wealthy in order to be well dressed! A woman needs three things in order to be attractively dressed:

1. A little money.
2. A lot of good taste.
3. A tremendous amount of imagination.

We must dress. Why not wear the colors and styles that are prettiest on us?

Good taste can be yours! Every month study carefully one or more of the fashion magazines. It takes so little time. Notice in detail the clothes shown, the accessories, the hemlines, hairdos, etc. This is the best way to keep up on what is new. A woman who has "good taste" can buy less expensive pieces of clothing, jewelry, shoes, and accessories, and look very expensively dressed. Remember that simplicity of line is important. A basic black dress with fashionable, well-fitting lines can be your dearest closet gem. A change of accessories can make it look like a new outfit each time. A bright red or figured dress, on the other hand, if it is worn a lot, will be remembered each time.

There are five basic colors: black, brown, navy, gray, and beige. Center your wardrobe around one of these colors. That is, if you choose black as your basic, you would have a basic black dress or suit, black shoes and purse and hat. The other colors included in your wardrobe look well with black. Of course, if you can afford it, it is nice to have more than one basic color in your wardrobe.

Discover your most flattering colors; venture into the yard goods department of your favorite department store. Locate a mirror and hold up various colored fabrics next to your face. Which are your best colors? Ask a friend's advice, if you like. *A well-rounded wardrobe is a planned wardrobe.* Never buy an article of clothing that will not fit into your present wardrobe. Take a wardrobe inventory and plan from there. Here are some miscellaneous hints on dressing in good taste.

44

- Is your hemline up to date?
- Avoid "gingerbread extras" of any kind.
- Only one kind of jewelry at a time; if your necklace or bracelet is pearl, your earrings must be too.
- Scale the size of your jewelry to your size.
- A minimum of jewelry, please—imaginative and dramatic. Perhaps *just* a pair of earrings, or *just* a bib necklace, or *just* a large sparkling pin.
- If you are "hip heavy," wear slim skirts and large collars.
- If your arms are too thin or too heavy, avoid sleeveless styles.
- Wear a good foundation garment.
- Seamless nylons.
- When you wear heels, wear gloves.
- Shoes and purse do match.
- Keep your eyes open for new ideas. Don't be afraid to be an individual. There's only one *you* in all the world. Make the most of *you*.
- Always dress neatly and attractively—twenty-four hours a day. Look fresh and feel fresh while you're going about your daily housework—a clean outfit on, hair combed, lipstick on. While your hair is up in curls, wrap a bright scarf around your head. Don't frighten the milkman and mailman or your *family*. You do want to look your best for those who matter most to you, don't you? Your sleep wear and lingerie should always be feminine, clean, and fresh. Keep fragrant sachet in your lingerie drawer. Enjoy being a woman!

Think for a moment how silly we would look if we walked down the street today wearing the same styles as those that were popular fifteen years ago.

Fashions do change and style favorites disappear, but our spiritual wardrobe will live on forever. How well dressed are you on the "inside?"

Colleen Townsend Evans, a former movie star, at one time had all of the physical beauty and material glamour a woman could ever desire, and yet she was keenly aware of a great void in her life. It seemed that she had always been seeking for an answer to life. At an early age she had an overwhelming desire to know God. She searched, she tried living a good, moral life, she tried to lose herself in Sunday school teaching and church activities, but all to no avail.

She became discouraged, and it was during this time that her picture appeared on the cover of a national magazine and she was offered a movie contract. While in Hollywood she attended a church retreat where she met six hundred young people who had already discovered what she was looking for. Their lives were different, they were "glowing" for their Lord. She wanted what they had, and she found what they had: a personal faith in the Savior, Jesus Christ. They had found victory because Christ had already won the victory. She became a "new creature" in Jesus Christ, as she learned to know, believe, and follow the King of kings.

She passed up many social engagements to attend Bible studies and prayer meetings. She loved having fellowship with God's children. Her testimony was beautiful. Christ could be seen in her. Today she is happily married to Rev. Louis Evans, and is the mother of four children. She knows that true beauty and true loveliness come from God. She has found the "peace that passeth understanding" and the greatest joy a human being can ever experience—through faith in Jesus Christ, the Beautiful Savior.

> *Let the Beauty of Jesus*
> *be seen in me,*
> *All of His wonderful*
> *passion and purity.*

B. D. ACKLEY

THE LOVELINESS OF CHRIST

Could we catch the glistening of the dew or snow-
*   flake,*
Or the rainbow colors painted on the clouds.
Add to these the brightness of the stars and moon-
*   light,*
And the mantle white which mountain peaks en-
*   shroud.*

Then, if we could catch the glitter of each jewel
*   from the earth, or gathered from the briny sea,*
Blend them all together in one mighty prism—
Still the loveliness of Christ is more to me.

He is altogether lovely, He's the fairest of the fair,
And on Him alone through life I can depend.
Oh, all language fails completely when I try to
*   tell the world*
Of the loveliness of Christ, my Lord and Friend.

HERBERT BUFFUM

48

CHAPTER FIVE

Crown your Husband!

YOUR husband is the king of your heart, the king of your home, and that is the way God would have it to be. Man was created for this role; he is strong and masculine; he is the provider for and the protector of his own little family. Did you know that the word "husband" is an Anglo-Saxon word which means "the master of the house?" A Christian husband rules with love, wisdom, and tenderness. It is up to us as wives, vice presidents, to keep Dad at the head of the house. One of the greatest tragedies of the American home is that wives are trying—and often with success—to step into the husband's pants. This is not God's way! The Bible clearly states, "For the husband is the head of the wife as Christ is the head of the church, . . . As the church is subject to Christ, so let the wives also be subject in everything to their husbands" (Ephesians 5:23, 24).

If God's order for the home is ignored, the results may be tragic. Dad himself will lose his self-esteem, his manly pride, his sense of fulfillment. The children, too, will suffer greatly. Some years ago an American judge wrote an article centered around the nine words that can stop juvenile delinquency: *Put Father Back at the Head of the Family.*

Young people must be taught to respect authority. A high school principal in Milan, Italy, had this to say, "The child who respects his father, and mother too, will respect his teachers, the laws of his country, the policemen, his elders."

Every time that we mothers overrule Dad, we undermine his authority and his standing in the eyes of the children, we knock a piece off the child's foundation. How carefully we must watch ourselves. If we could understand that much of our importance as mothers lies in building up Dad's image before the children, we would receive a much deeper satisfaction from our calling. Let's keep Dad at the head of the home! Crown him king of your heart and king of your home!

Treat your husband like a king, and he will treat you like his queen; do everything in the world to make him happy, and you can be sure he'll do the same for you in return. It just works that way!

Don't try to domesticate him. Certainly, most men like to flip pancakes or barbecue steaks; and they take pride in doing the "man's work" around the home. Be sure to show your appreciation when your husband helps you out. It's easy for wives to forget that husbands work hard at their jobs, too. A man's home must be his castle.

Little things mean a lot! When he comes home at the end of the day, be ready. Look your prettiest for the one you most want to impress. Your hair is combed, you're neatly dressed, your lipstick is on and, of course, you're wearing your brightest smile. The children are clean, and the house is tidy. The table is set and, doesn't dinner smell delicious?

Greet your husband with a loving kiss and warm enthusiasm. A wise wife, instinctively tactful, avoids the jarring news that the washer broke down, or that the checking account doesn't balance, or that she got a parking ticket, until *after* dinner. She does not bother Dad with any of the daily discipline problems which she should have handled at the time they occurred. Once the king has reached his castle, he needs time to remove his working suit of armor. Greet your husband like this, and he'll be whispering deep down inside every night, "There's no place like home; how I love my wonderful wife! I'm the luckiest man in the world."

Husbands need tender care. They need well-balanced, nutritious meals attractively served in a relaxed setting. Fix his favorites; whip up special culinary surprises for him, and watch him light up. You know the old saying, "The quickest way to a man's heart is through his stomach." Study the cookbooks, clip recipes, practice setting a lovely, inviting table. Every once in a while treat yourselves to a late dinner by candlelight—just the two of you. You'll know it's worth every effort when your husband leans back, smiles at you with a twinkle in his eye and says, "Honey, that was the best dinner I've had in a long time."

Fuss over your husband, fetch his slippers if you like, take his advice, pamper him to your heart's content. It's a game you'll both enjoy. Encourage him in every way. He needs you to give him the big boost in life that a man must have to be a success, to be completely happy.

Learn to enjoy and understand the things your husband likes and does. Be "good friends," have fun together, "date" often. Many couples who were once so in love they fairly flew to the altar, now look at one another and say, "We've grown apart." They've allowed housekeeping, child raising, a job, and even friends to keep them from maintaining a home paradise. A happy marriage is not an accident; it is the result of much effort.

In our modern world we are caught up in life's whirlwinds. The husband is carried off to his business interests, the wife to her home and children. The only answer is that each must give a little and develop a keener interest in the other's world, so that the two worlds will become one, revolving in beautiful harmony. A husband must confide in his wife; she is not a mere ornament in the home. She is his helpmeet in all the affairs of life. *Together* share your dreams, your hopes, your plans, and ideas. *Together* enjoy the precious little antics your children perform. *Together* appreciate God's world, nature, picnics, Sunday afternoon rides and hikes. *Together* dive into the rich world of music, art, and beauty. Focus attention on your *common* interests and develop them *together*. A family is not a group of individuals; it is a group of individuals doing things together. In the "old days" life was simpler, families found it easy to do things together. Today we just "do things." When a family stops doing things together, it almost ceases to be a family, and trouble inevitably begins. Have you ever heard of the dreadful "separitis" diseases?

Disease 1. Quarrels, bickering, harsh and cutting words, tears.

REMEDY:

Place family on its knees, set the open Bible before Dad's knees, cover all wounds with much prayer, lean fully upon the Great Physician. Repeat this treatment daily, adding family church worship, Sunday school, picnics, laughter, and lots of love and patience.

Disease 2. Moody child, one who sulks and pouts and complains.

REMEDY:

A battered football helmet applied to boy's head. Add one Dad and a football and place in an open, grassy area, and stir well for an hour. Continue the treatment until all symptoms have vanished. As one pastor said, "I'd rather have an aching back now, than an aching heart later."

We "up-to-date" young marrieds contend that the saying, "The family that prays together stays together" is old fashioned. God help us to be old fashioned!

Peter Marshall explained married love in a most beautiful way: "We are souls living in bodies. Therefore, when we really fall in love, it isn't just a physical attraction. If it's just that, it won't last. Ideally, it's also a spiritual attraction. God has opened our eyes and let us see into someone's soul. We have fallen in love with the inner person, the person who is going to live forever. That's why God is the greatest asset to romance. He thought it up in the first place. Include Him in every part of your marriage, and He will lift it above the level of the mundane to something rare and beautiful and lasting."

From *A Man Called Peter*. Used by permission of McGraw-Hill Book Company, Inc.

LETTER TO DADDIES

Dearest Daddies,

We, as mommies, do solemnly promise to crown you as the kings of our hearts and homes. But *please,* daddies, help us. How can you help? By making us your queens, that's how. If we know that we are loved, and appreciated, and respected, and understood, our desires to make you happy will know no limitations.

O, we know that we females are funny creatures! Man has known that for a long, long time. Women want to be little girls at times, leaning heavily on their strong husbands; at other times they want to be independent, mature women, who like to think and act independently; they want so to be kind and patient and loving mommies and homebodies, and at the same time they want to be glamorous sweethearts who like to be "courted." You have a real job on your hands, daddies, when it comes to understanding us. But do keep trying. The rewards are tremendous!

What were the things your wife loved so about you before you were married? Are those traits still there? Oh, we know that marriage cannot always be a "pink-cloud" type of co-existence; but, if it isn't to some degree a lifelong courtship, bushels and bushels of happiness will be missing from your marriage. Kiss your wife in the morning, when you come home from work, and for no special reason at all. She may faint from shock the first time you kiss her for no apparent reason, but watch her spirits soar!

When she has worked hard to prepare your favorite dish, bubble over with sincere appreciation. Even her cooking will improve, if she knows her efforts are really appreciated. In some ways you must use the same psychology on us that you use on children: compliment us on the good things we do, and try to pay as little attention as possible to the things we do that aren't quite up to par.

We realize that you just *expect* your home to be clean and neat—that you take this for granted. But, when a wife has been scrubbing, polishing, waxing, and dusting all day long, and she tells her husband so, just a few grateful words, such as, "Dear, it looks wonderful!" will mean more to her than you can imagine.

It's so good to be loved, even when we're not lovable. There are days when the children have been behaving like a tribe of wild Indians, and things have gone wrong all day; company is coming for dinner, and mommy is almost in pieces. Her nerves are shattered. Lend a hand, daddy, dress the children for her, or just take them for a walk, so she can have a little peace and quiet to prepare herself and her meal for the guests. The less you say at a time like this, the better it is. The Bible, in its great wisdom, instructs us: "A soft answer turns away wrath." And when those tangles do come, be quick to kiss and make up. So many couples stay angry for hours simply because they don't know how to make up gracefully. A kiss, a smile—that's all it takes.

I heard not long ago of a wise and happy wife who came to the door after a very trying day to greet her husband. She kissed him and said, "Are you terribly tired tonight, dear?" "No," he replied cautiously. "Then

57

I think I'd like to be," she said, as she leaned on his shoulder. This is the kind of love and understanding that makes a marriage beautiful.

Little things mean so much more to women than they do to men. We are true romanticists! An unexpected phone call, an inexpensive piece of jewelry, an invitation out to dinner, an appreciative word, a tender expression of love—these are the "little things" that will add glitter to your queen's crown. We love you, daddies. You are the kings. We want so to be your queens!

Lovingly,

Mommies

Husbands, love your wives, as Christ loved the church and gave himself for her (Ephesians 5:25).

CHAPTER SIX

The Tender Care of "Jesus' Little Lambs"

Y OUR children, Jesus' little lambs,—just love, love, love them with all your hearts. Our children can forget and forgive our failures, even our unreasonableness, our moodiness, and our crossness, but they can never forget evidences that they are not loved. Love is as essential to our children as the food they eat and the air they breathe. Children can never be satisfied without love. Give your child all the love he needs.

In the breast of the bulb is the promise of spring;
In the little blue egg there's a bird that will sing;
In the soul of the seed is the hope of the sod;
In the heart of a child is the kingdom of God.

WILLIAM STIGER
Youth's Favorite Poems, III, 23

I often look at my children and think of the line Emerson wrote, "All I have seen teaches me to trust the Creator for all I have not seen."

To have a child is one of the greatest privileges a woman can ever know. Mothers are not necessarily made when the child is born. There is a great difference between merely bearing children and becoming a mother in the truest sense of the word. The primary attribute of motherhood is love. Someone has said, "Before I could understand all the words I heard I knew that 'God is love'—not in so many words, of course, but by the look in my mother's eyes, the sound of her voice, the smile on her face."

I'm afraid most of us must hang our heads a little when we ask ourselves if our children will be able to say that about us. Most mothers must readily admit that they do not measure up to the standards of the *ideal mother.* I know that I fall short in so many ways. But I believe that our God knows and understands the desires of our hearts, and He forgives our failures, if we but ask Him.

How important it is to spend lots and lots of time with our children—reading to them, talking to them, listening to them, playing games with them, singing to them; you know, these years when they are young are so precious; I hope we don't have to ask ourselves, with tears in our eyes, a few years from now, "Why, oh why, didn't I spend more time with my dear children when they were young and needed me so?"

But, of course, we must let them exert their independence, and express themselves and their individuality, too. Our children want not only to love us, but they also want to respect us. Discipline must play a definite part in a Christian home. I mean the kind of discipline that is firm but friendly. When you say something, mean it. Stick to it! You and your husband must stand as a united front; you must make decisions regarding your children *together.* If you do have differences of

61

opinion concerning the way a situation should be handled, *please* be wise enough to discuss it when you and your husband are alone, and never in front of the children. All of these things work together to give your child a sense of security which will be of immeasurable value to him all the days of his life.

We are so proud of our children that we can hardly contain ourselves at times. It is hard for us to realize that our children's antics, which seem so hilarious to us, might not be quite so interesting to others. We must be careful not to talk too much about our children to others. Save those "cute" stories for Dad, Grandma and Grandpa, and close friends who have small children of their own.

When you do talk about your children, be careful, if they are within ear range. Pity the poor mother who says to a friend in front of little Billy, "Oh, dear! I don't know what I'm going to do with Billy! He's so wild and naughty that I'm just worn to a frazzle. I don't know what to try next." And there sits little Billy, horns creeping higher, thinking to himself, "Heh, heh—  have I got her in a frenzy! Wild I am—wild I'll be!" You see, it is true with children as it is of adults: we are what we are expected to be—in many ways. If that mother would have been wise, she would have said something like this, "I enjoy taking Billy visiting with me, he is such a gentleman!" Billy is thinking, "Who? Me? I am? Sure I am!" And chances are he will be. Don't ever underestimate the capacity of those little minds.

Read down-to-earth books on understanding your children. We must be well acquainted with each of our children, their dreams, their fears, their hopes, their ideas. I heard of a mother of four children who took time every week to go for a long walk with each of her children individually, so that she could really understand each one better. I think it's wise to try to put ourselves in our child's position every once in a while. Let's try it now. You know how it is when you are as busy as a bee and your child comes to you with a long story of a little incident which seems completely insignificant to you. You haven't time really to listen. Now, be your child. Here is something that happened that made a deep impression on you. It's important to you, and you want to share it with the one who loves you most, your mother. Imagine the hurt when she isn't even interested enough to listen to you. Tell me, mother, how do you feel when another adult shows no apparent interest at all in what you're saying? It hurts, doesn't it? Yes, I sincerely believe we'd all be better mothers if we would try to think and feel as our children do.

Have you ever tried "deputizing" those little cowboys or cowgirls? Children love responsibility, if it's given to them in the right way. Your words of praise for a job well done mean more to your children than dozens of expensive toys. Be grateful for your child's little acts of kindness. Put confidence in your child.

Allow him to help you make the beds, dust and vacuum, if he likes to. I know that it will take a little longer, but, believe me, every minute you "waste" during times like this is returned to you a hundred fold. Your "thank you's," smiles, winks, kisses, and hugs—in gratitude or for no special reason at all—are *priceless* treasures in the eyes of the "little lambs" which God has entrusted to you.

Let *kindness* be the motto of your home. Outdo one another in showing kindness and consideration, and you can be sure that your children will grow up to be happy, well adjusted, fruitful human beings. Don't confuse kindness with softness, however. You want your son to go in there and block and tackle at a football game with all of his energy and enthusiasm; but you also want him to give his opponent a helping hand after the whistle has blown. Kindness as an everyday habit leads to successful and happy growth in children.

Whatever it is that you want your child to be and say and do tomorrow, you must be and say and do today. Whatever your child sees and hears you do, that he has every right to do. It's not just what we say, it's *how* we say it. Our responsibility is overwhelming.

A father decided to go off to the corner tavern on a cold, wintry Saturday afternoon. Slipping quietly from his house, he started down the snow-covered street toward his destination. He hadn't gone far before he heard a voice behind him. It was his six-year-old son who said, "Go ahead, Daddy, I'm just following in your footsteps." But daddy didn't go right ahead. The child's innocent remark took on great significance to that father. He turned to his son and tenderly picked him up in his strong arms and said, "Son, from this day forward, my footsteps will lead you to only the right places." And they went home together—a father and his son.

Yes, children have big eyes and big ears. The example of parents is the most important book which children can read. A little girl watched her mother slip into her bedroom every day for several minutes. When she came out a heavenly peace glowed in her eyes. This little girl was being trained in a life of prayer. I often ask myself, as I lie down on my pillow at night, What have I recorded today on the impressionable minds of my young sons? God forgive our failures! And He does! The wonder of it all is that He loves us enough to forgive us time and time again.

> *If we confess our sins, he is*
> *faithful and just, and will forgive*
> *our sins and cleanse us from*
> *all unrighteousness* (1 John 1:9).

There are times when I wonder how God can forgive me when I fail Him in so many ways. And then I think of perhaps the most beautiful illustration I have ever heard, and I feel secure under His mighty wing.

The illustration goes something like this: The son of a devoted Christian mother and father had turned his back on God and his parents, and had gone out to make his way in the world. He succeeded. He became quite famous as an entertainer, and was doing very well for himself, until liquor took hold of him. Before long he was a penniless alcoholic, on the verge of suicide. As he stood on the bridge, trying to find the courage to jump, he thought of his parents, and longed to be back with them just once more. But his father had died— brokenhearted—and his mother was alone now. He grabbed onto the last glimmer of hope, and wrote to his mother, telling her that the next day he would be on the 12:05 train going through his home town. His mother's house was facing the railroad tracks, so he told her that if she would forgive him and wanted him home again, she should tie a white handkerchief on the front limb of the tree in the front yard. If the handkerchief was there, he would get off the train; if it wasn't on the tree, he would keep right on going.

He borrowed money for his train fare. The train was pulling into his home town. His heart was pounding,

66

his hands were perspiring, eagerly he leaned forward in his seat hoping, hoping, hoping to see the white handkerchief on the limb of the tree.

And then it happened! It was almost too much for him to bear. He wept unashamedly. Not only was there a white handkerchief, but also dozens of white towels, pillow cases, white shirts, and even sheets hanging all over the yard. And there was mother, waving white towels with both hands. Welcome home, my son, welcome home!

And, this is just the way our loving God forgives us when we ask for forgiveness. He always welcomes us home. Yes, we are precious children in God's sight. He longs to finish in us the work He has begun.

When you begin to lose patience with your children, think of God's great patience toward us. When you become too busy to demonstrate your love for your little ones, remember that our great God always has time for us and love for us—love so great that He was willing to make the supreme sacrifice for us. When we fail to understand our children's problems, we need to consider our heavenly Father's great understanding toward us and our problems.

CHILDREN OF THE HEAVENLY FATHER

*Children of the heavenly Father
Safely in His bosom gather;
Nestling bird nor star in heaven
Such a refuge e'er was given.*

God His own doth tend and nourish,
In His holy courts they flourish.
From all evil things He spares them,
In His mighty arms He bears them.

Neither life nor death shall ever
From the Lord His children sever;
Unto them His grace He showeth,
And their sorrows all He knoweth.

Though He giveth or He taketh,
God His children ne'er forsaketh,
His the loving purpose solely
To preserve them pure and holy.

Carolina Vilhelmina (Sandell) Berg
Tr. Ernst William Olson

Have you ever looked lovingly down upon your child as he slept peacefully in his bed, and wondered how such an angel could possibly have hit his sister over the head with a book, and broken your favorite vase only a few hours earlier? There is a theological expression which reads in the Latin, *simul justus et peccator,* which in our language means, "at the same time sinner and saint." Perhaps this will help us better to understand the conflict which each of us faces in life, children and adults alike.

68

THE TEACHER'S PRAYER

My Lord, I do not ask to stand
As king or prince of high degree.
I only pray, that hand in hand,
A child and I may come to Thee.

To teach a tender voice to pray
Two childish eyes Thy face to see,
Two feet to guide in Thy straight way—
This fervently I ask of Thee.

O grant Thy patience to impart
Thy holy law, Thy words of truth;
Give, Lord, Thy grace that my whole heart
May overflow with love for youth.

As step by step we tread the way,
Trusting and confident and free—
A child and I, day by day,
Find sweet companionship with Thee.

> Norman E. Richardson,
> *Youth's Favorite Poems*, V, 21

Let's tuck our children in bed now, shall we? They've had their baths, pajamas are buttoned, teeth are brushed, and they're now ready for their bedtime story. About that story—do use all of your bottled up imagination, mother. Make up little stories that have not only lessons in them, but stories that will lead your little lambs closer to the Shepherd.

Here's a story that my boys love; so bring your little ones close and I will begin:

Once upon a time a happy family lived in a cozy little home near the woods. There was a mommy, a daddy, and two little boys named Raymie and Rickie. Their mommy had told them *never* to go into the woods alone. Now, these boys were good boys, and they obeyed their mommy and daddy; but, one day when they were playing ball in the yard, Raymie threw the ball too hard, and it went rolling into the woods. Raymie and Rickie forgot what their mommy had told them, and went running into the woods after the ball. Oh my, but they did have a fine time! They saw squirrels and rabbits and chipmunks and even a skunk. They were having such a good time that they didn't even notice how dark it was getting. Raymie looked up and said, "Oh, oh! It's getting dark, Rickie; we'd better hurry home before Mommy gets worried about us." He took his brother's hand, and they started to walk. They went one way and then they tried another way and another way. But, they couldn't find their way out of the woods. They were lost!

It was dark now, and the old owl in the tree said, "Whoo, whoo, whoo." The little boys were frightened, and they sat down under a tree and began to cry. And then Raymie remembered what his mother had told him. She had said, "Jesus always hears and answers our prayers." So little Raymie bowed his head and prayed, "Dear Jesus, please help us now to get home to Mommy and Daddy. Amen." And soon a hunter came along and picked the boys up in his strong arms and brought them home to their mommy and daddy. Oh! How glad they were to see their boys! They had been so worried and they, too, had been praying that God would bring their boys safely home.

That night when they were saying their prayers, Raymie and Rickie thanked the dear Lord Jesus for answering their prayer.

When they had finished their prayers, Raymie and Rickie looked up at their mommy and daddy and said, "We will never, never go into the woods again. We will always obey you—honest, 'cause you know what's best for us."

Did you like that story? I hope so. And now it's time to say your prayers, little ones.

> *Dear Father, whom I cannot see,*
> *Smile down from heaven on little me.*
> *Let angels through the darkness spread*
> *Their holy wings around my bed,*
> *And keep me safe, because I am*
> *My loving Shepherd's little lamb. Amen.*

Goodnight, darlings!

What? All right; I'll bring you a drink of water.

CHAPTER SEVEN

Your Home —

Your Paradise!

YOUR home is meant to be your paradise, your husband's paradise, and your children's paradise! Your home can be a little bit of heaven right here on earth, if the Great Carpenter has built your home. Unless the Lord builds, the home fails. Yes, the Lord loves to build homes; He was once a carpenter in Nazareth, and He is still a carpenter, building spiritual homes. His materials are love, joy, peace, kindness, goodness, faithfulness, self-control and *you, your husband,* and *your children.* The homes He builds never wear out; they grow stronger, brighter and better as the years go by.

We wouldn't think of building a stone fireplace without stones, or of baking an apple pie without apples. Why then are so many people trying to build Christian homes without Christ? They try to maintain "Christian" principles, establish a "Christian" home, and even use "Christian" terminology; but, without the very presence of Christ there cannot be a Christian home. The great and holy God must be *living* in that home, He must be *living* in the hearts of those who call that house "home."

A gala society banquet was held one fall evening in a large eastern city. A famous broadway actor was the guest of honor. The elderly and frail neighborhood pastor was a guest also. Toward the close of the program the actor was called upon to recite the Twenty-third Psalm. His voice was perfect, his expression was moving, his enunciation, flawless. When he had finished the audience's applause rang through the auditorium. Some even gave him a standing ovation.

The elderly pastor was also asked to recite the Twenty-third Psalm. There he stood, slightly hunched over, only a few silver white hairs gracing the top of his head; and he began in a quiet, cracked voice. When he had finished, not one person clapped; the auditorium was silent, the people motionless. Tears were running down many cheeks. It was the famous actor, with tears in his own eyes, who stood to his feet, walked over to the elderly pastor, shook his hand and said, "Sir, I know the psalm, you know the Shepherd."

74

The Lord is my shepherd, I shall not want;
he makes me lie down in green pastures.
He leads me beside still waters;
he restores my soul.
He leads me in paths of righteousness
for his name's sake.

Even though I walk throught the valley of the
shadow of death,
I fear no evil;
for thou art with me;
thy rod and thy staff,
they comfort me.

Thou preparest a table before me
in the presence of my enemies;
thou anointest my head with oil,
my cup overflows.
Surely goodness and mercy shall follow me
all the days of my life;
and I shall dwell in the house of the Lord
for ever.

Psalm 23

How is it in your home? Do you know about Christianity, or do you know Christ personally?

HOME DECORATING

God has given us each his own personality. Our personalities should be expressed in our homes. Does your home express you, your way of life, your ideas? Of course, the different members of your family will have their own ideas on what they like in their home; compromise, however, is the answer and the beauty of the Christian home.

Of course, we as mothers usually have more interest in home furnishings; but we should certainly honor our family's ideas. As a family, do you like the gracious lines of French or Italian provincial, or do you long for the dramatic and clean look of contemporary, or do you enjoy the informal warmth of Early American? Many leading decorators agree that furniture from various periods may be tastefully combined in the same room.

What kind of life do you live? Do you like informal entertaining, barbecues, late coffee parties? Or is your life simpler? Or perhaps more formal? Your home should meet the needs of your way of life. Let's talk about the various rooms.

Living room. This is the room that gives our guests their first impression of our home, the room that speaks of the "mood" of the entire home—perhaps our most important room. Here you will entertain, relax, read, listen to music, converse. Are the chairs comfortable? Can you read easily by the lamps you have? Do *you* think it is an inviting room? Is your family's taste expressed in this room?

Dining room. Keep in mind that the living room and the dining room are always related. Plenty of storage space here for your finest dishes? Is there ample room for successful entertaining? Here is an excellent place to experiment (if your husband is so inclined) with various lighting effects. By the way, have you tried the new pastel-tone light bulbs? They can give such a soft and pretty glow to your rooms; do be certain that they complement the color scheme in the room. I hope the centerpiece on your dining room table is a beautiful conversation piece. Let your artistic, creative nature creep out, and do experiment with various seasonal arrangements for your dining-room table and for the other rooms as well. Candlelight and flowers always make a beautiful setting for a dinner party or buffet supper.

Family room. I think the "family room" idea is an excellent one. A place really to kick off your shoes, spread the newspaper out, watch TV, and write letters. Perhaps a desk in here for Junior and Dad to do their "homework" on. Bookshelves, too, with lots of good reading material. Above all else, be sure the family room is livable in every way.

Kitchen. Beautiful surroundings can make your kitchen hours more fun. Plan your kitchen decorations as carefully as you plan your living-room decor. A kitchen should be the happiest room in the house. A "happy looking" kitchen can do a lot to keep you happy as you work. It can help to start your family off to a bright day, and will be the setting for many sunny family hours. Bright, washable wallpaper, crispy curtains, easy-to-clean counters and floors, clever little accessories that can be useful as well as decorative—all ideas for that "happy" kitchen. Plan for convenience, too, and plan for lots and lots of handy shelf and drawer space. Has any woman ever had too much shelf space? I doubt it!

Bathroom. Clean, fresh, pretty, spring-like—this best expresses my idea of the ideal bathroom. Use an interesting decorating theme here and carry it out well, whether it be poodles, flowers, or just an unusual color scheme.

Bedrooms. A bedroom is meant for *relaxing.* The decorating scheme must *be* relaxing. Soft colors, soft lights, a comfortable bed and fluffy rugs to wriggle your toes in on a cold winter morning all will add to the relaxed "feel" of your bedroom. Plenty of drawer and closet space? Since the bedroom is also the dressing room, there must be good mirrors and plenty of privacy.

Children's room. Your fun-loving youngsters should be able to have the time of their lives in their own room, their paradise. This is their playroom, rumpus room, and fun room. This is the place to have those messes, and not in the living room or kitchen for the rest of the family to fall over. If you teach your children this in a kindly way, it will not only be a help to you, but it will also be excellent training for the children. They will learn respect for property. If they are taught at home to respect mother's possessions and to keep the front room neat, you will find it much easier to take them out socially. Of course, one can go overboard on this, too. Do keep in mind that children should certainly feel comfortable in any room in your home; but when it comes to playtime and/or roughhousing, corral it in *their* room.

Children like to take pride in their room. Consider your child's likes and dislikes when you decorate. If you have a little girl who loves dolls, a very feminine setting for the little miss; if you have boys who are junior size cowboys, space pilots, or circus performers, decorate to please them. Lots of color, life, and gaiety! *Washable* paints and wallpapers, rugs, and fabrics, plenty of shelf space and a roomy toy box, so your youngsters can learn to take pride in their room by keeping it neat between play sessions. Remember this is your children's room. Decorate to please them.

Decorating need not be expensive; new paint, a few attractive decorator pillows, new lamp shades, a slip cover, a few new accessories, or a lovely arrangement of flowers might be all you need to turn your average home into something way above average. Try tiling the tops of your old end tables or coffee tables, spraypaint your old bedroom set in a pretty pastel-colored rough-texture paint. Or how about wood-paneling that area above the fireplace, or redoing your picture frames in antique white? Ideas you have; ideas you must use. Read and study at least one good home decorating magazine every month. Clip and file pictures of room decors that catch your eye, and page through decorating books from the library. Many department and furniture stores have a decorating service, if you desire professional advice.

Color alone can make a world of difference in your home. Here are a few ideas to keep in mind when you're working with color:

- Your *favorite* colors should be tastefully brought out in your home.

- One strong pattern is enough for any room. Keep your room color scheme simple and dramatic, your colors few but carefully selected.

- Some colors are cool, others are warm. Warmth is suggested by reds, yellows—colors of the fire and sun. Cool colors are blues, greens—the colors of the grass and sky.

- Some colors "pounce," others recede. Bold colors do pounce; they bring objects closer. Subdued colors recede, give a spacious feeling to a room. Closely-blending colors conceal. If your room is small, light, subdued colors will make it appear larger. But don't forget a few vital bold accents, will you? Plan about two thirds of your room in one predominant color. Unequal amounts of color are more pleasing.

- Don't ever be afraid of color. Use it artistically, just as God, the Great Artist, did when He created this beautiful world we live in.

Your home is your paradise: no matter how old or how new, how small or how large; let it reveal you, your family, and most important of all—your faith. Do the pictures on your walls, the music on your piano, the magazines on your table witness to your visitors of your faith in Jesus Christ as Lord of your life and home?

So long as there are homes to which men turn at the close of the day;

So long as there are homes where children are, where women stay,

If love and loyalty and faith be found across these sills—

A stricken nation can recover from its gravest ills.

GRACE NOLL CROWELL,
Youth's Favorite Poems, III, 12

HOUSEWORK!

Okay, mothers, let's tackle this business of housework! I know what you're probably thinking, Ugh! Do you ever think, while in the midst of a pile of dirty dishes, with beds still to make, and children to dress, and ironing staring at you as well as a messy house,

"Wasn't I made for better things than this?" And, if we listen, the answer seems to echo and re-echo through the house: The routine work we do in our homes every day makes life secure and happy and orderly for those we love the most. The biggest hurdle we have to cross is our approach to our daily tasks.

Thank God every morning that you have something to do that day, whether you like it or not. Being forced to do that work and forced to do your best, will breed in you temperance, self-control, diligence, and strength of will, cheerfulness, and contentment, and a hundred other virtues which the idle will never know.

CHARLES KINGSLEY

"I cannot do much," said a little star,
"to make the dark world bright;
My silver beams cannot travel far
Through the folding gloom of night.
But I'm only a part of God's great plan,
And I'll cheerfully do the best I can."

AUTHOR UNKNOWN

The Word of God gives us the highest motivation of all when it tells us, "And whatsoever you do, in word or in deed, do all in the name of the Lord Jesus, giving thanks to God the Father through him" (Colossians 3:17).

Yes, mothers, if we think of our work in the light of this verse, then life becomes rich and glorious, even though it is spent among humble surroundings, and even if it does seem very monotonous at times.

Enjoy housework! It *is* rewarding; you can see the results of your efforts. Always take great pride in your home, and your home will show it. We can talk ourselves into and out of a lot of things in life. For example, if you tell yourself, "Ugh! I hate housework!" believe me, you will—you will! But, if you say with a smile, "I'm going to whiz through my housework today; it'll be such a good feeling to have everything clean and orderly in my little home," you'll be amazed at how much easier and more fun housework will be.

There are ways to make housework easier, so let's think about these ideas that will make housework as painless as possible. System is a key word. You must have a systematic plan for keeping your home at its sparkling best. Before you go to bed at night, put the newspaper away, straighten out the chairs, hang up clothes, and if you feel up to it, quickly dust off the table tops. What a wonderful feeling to wake up in the morning to find your living and dining rooms spotlessly clean. You're off on the right foot. Now, wash your face, comb your hair, put on a little lipstick, and you're ready to fix and enjoy a delicious breakfast with your family. (You are wearing a pretty duster, aren't you?) Be the morning sunshine, mother! After breakfast take a few minutes to start the day with God as a family.

I'd like to suggest the daily promise box for morning devotions. Each member of the family takes part, because each one reads the verse he has selected. Begin the day with prayer. Martin Luther once said he was so busy that he had to get up several hours earlier, so he would have ample time to spend in prayer at the beginning of the day. Many families find that the best time to have the family altar is after supper, since they have more time together then. Of course you, as a family, must decide on the best time for your own devotions. The important thing is that you do take time together to read God's Word, perhaps thoughts from a daily devotional book, and then talk to your heavenly Father in prayer. We must never become too busy to take time out for the daily family altar. This is the greatest need of our modern world. Only when we put God first will our lives remain in perfect balance.

After breakfast dress the children, send your husband off to work with a big smile and a loving kiss, and prepare to fly through your housework. I thoroughly enjoy background music while I work (in fact, I enjoy good music just about any time). Music in the background keeps a melody on my lips and a song in my heart. The dishes, the beds, the bathroom, dusting, polishing, and vacuuming. Time out for coffee! And now decide what your project for the morning will be: ironing, mending, closet cleaning, letter writing, or whatever.

Some women find it helpful to write out a list of things they'd like to get done during that day. If this helps you, by all means do it. I do it occasionally, but I find that there are times when the pressure to get things done is a little too great. But do keep a running list of household needs (aspirin, toothpaste, bandages, etc.) and also a running grocery list. Add to these lists when other items come to mind. This is such a help! A housewife has to be an efficiency expert as well as a good administrator, and practice makes perfect.

Now, let's toss around a few ideas about the various household tasks. Are you with me?

Dishwashing. I don't especially enjoy doing dishes, so I have disciplined myself to do up the dishes as soon as dinner is over. I never leave dishes stacked, and it works out very well for me. In order to save time, I let my daily dishes drip dry with the exception of silver- ware and glasses. I've heard that this is even more sanitary. It sounds good anyway, doesn't it? With the terrific new dishwashing soaps, dishes sparkle without wiping, and your hands stay soft and lovely. Keep a bottle of hand lotion near the kitchen sink; when you have finished with the dishes, dry your hands and put lotion on them immediately.

Bedmaking. Smooth beds! Keep your spreads clean and fresh looking, and carefully place some pretty decorative pillows which blend in with your color scheme on your bed. Save time by ironing only pillow cases and, if you wish, the widest hem of the sheet. A little starch keeps your linens crisp.

Dusting. Don't push the dust around! Use a dust spray which collects the dust and adds a shine to your furniture. The same holds true when it comes to dusting your floors. Shiny floors, furniture, mirrors, and windows are the mark of a good housekeeper.

Scrubbing. There are many modern effort savers that can be used, but for my own part I like to get right down there on my knees when I scrub, and really get the job done well. Good exercise, too. Use a cleaning solution that doesn't require rinsing. We're lucky to be living in a day when there are so many good cleaning products to chose from.

Waxing. An inexpensive little waxer helps to give your floors an even glow. A colorless floor wax will not yellow your floors, but will keep them true to color. Go over your waxed floors when necessary with a lukewarm sponge. Whenever you really want to scrub a floor, you will find it necessary to rewax.

Vacuuming. Make use of all your attachments for cleaning woodwork, upholstery, lamps, even the inside of the car. If you have a cannister type vacuum, let it run—nozzle off—for several minutes in each room. This will help to collect a lot of dust in the air.

Kitchen grooming. Do your kitchen fixtures gleam? Is your sink scoured with cleanser after each dish washing session? Is your stove cleaned often? Is your refrigerator orderly and clean on the inside? Is it frost free? Are your cupboards well arranged? Do you store many regular cupboard items (brown sugar, powdered sugar, marshmallows, raisins, nuts, etc.) in tightly sealed plastic containers which help foods retain their original texture and flavor? A pretty little centerpiece on the kitchen table? If you can answer "Yes" to all these questions, you didn't need to read this paragraph.

Bathroom. Scour it every day. Keep all medicines as far away from children as possible. I can't emphasize this enough. Better to be safe than sorry any day. A thoughtful homemaker always has plenty of fresh towels (nicely arranged), soap, and a little can of a scented deodorant spray in the bathroom. A colorful bouquet is an extra plus for your bathroom.

Picking up. Most of us do more than our share of this, don't we? Not just for the children, but for the "king" as well. At least, we can train the children; all we can do with the king is try. If, as I suggested before, you have taught your youngsters to keep their messes in their own room, you have this problem pretty well under control. Pick up their things at nap time and bed time. Teach them to help. Make a game of it; do it together. Whenever your child does pick up his things, let the praises roll.

Washing and drying clothes. If you have an automatic washer and dryer, there isn't much more to tell you, except to be thankful. If you don't have a washer and dryer, try a little "sour grapes" rationalizing. You know, it can be helpful at times. While you're hanging clothes outdoors, instead of feeling sorry for yourself because you don't have a dryer, try talking to yourself. Tell yourself how fresh your clothes will smell when they're dried outdoors. Remind yourself how lucky you are to have a chance to get a little fresh air. This type of thinking works. I know!

Meal planning. Round up your recipe box, recipe books, paper and pencil, and sit down once a week to write out a tentative weekly menu. From this menu write out your grocery list carefully. Once a day your family must have a "semi-feast," including meat, potatoes, vegetables, salad, beverage, and dessert. Use variety in your menu planning. Try new recipes often. The people to experiment on are the members of your family (they love you anyway), not your guests. If the new recipe meets family approval, then spring it on your guests. Try new salads, vegetable casseroles, and combinations; make up your own hot dish recipes; try a spectacular dessert. Every once in a while ask your family what "special" dish they're in the mood for (homemade chili? waffles? a traditional delicacy? a foreign favorite? or whatever). Aim to please. Eat well-balanced, nutritious meals, and you'll all be feeling tip top. The money you spend on good food you save on doctor bills.

Now, this list of household jobs could go on indefinitely: closet and drawer cleaning, woodwork, walls, mending, baking; but I feel we've covered enough ground, so we'll stop right here.

What a schedule we mothers have! How do we do it all? Run here! Run there! Hurry through this and that! Rush, rush, rush.

LIFE, TWENTIETH CENTURY

Gadget, gadget, gadget,
Button, lever, hook.
Push! Turn! Pull!
Stop! Look! Go!
Is this to live?

What a spectacle we must present to our loving Creator, with all our fussing and fuming about. What an insult to our God to worry and fret so over our temporary earthly cares that we become too busy to be concerned over things eternal.

No time for God? What fools we are to clutter up
Our lives with common things
And leave without heart's gate
The Lord of life and Life itself—our God.
No time for God? Some day you'll lay aside
This mortal self and make your way
To worlds unknown,
And when you meet Him face to face,
Will He, should He, have time for you?

> *Youth's Favorite Poems*, IV, 17
> NORMAN L. TROTT

At times I can almost picture our Lord quietly shaking His head, looking down upon us with love and pity.

."Dear Lord and Father of mankind,
Forgive our foolish ways!
Reclothe us in our rightful mind,
In purer lives Thy service find,
In deeper reverence, praise . . .

"Take from our souls the strain and stress,
And let our ordered lives confess
The beauty of thy peace."

We must pause every day to enjoy the healing balm of Gilead, to find refreshment for body and soul. I find that the days I become "too busy" to take time to be alone with God are the hardest days. Try something— for just one week take fifteen minutes every day to be alone with God—to read the Bible, to pray, to meditate. If you do this, I can promise you that this week will be one of the most inspiring and uplifting weeks of your life. I'll promise you something else, too. Once you have felt the great store of strength, power, love, and patience which you receive from these moments with the Lord, you will never stop meeting Him alone each day—you talking to Him and He talking to you— a beautiful fellowship that only His children can know. We must slow down so that we will take time to find His holy will for us. We need to relax so we can gather together the strength and courage to do His bidding.

DAY BY DAY

I heard a voice at evening softly say:
Bear not thy yesterday into to-morrow,
Nor load this week with last week's load of sorrow;
Lift all thy burdens as they come, nor try
To weigh the present with the by and by.
One step, and then another, take thy way—
Live day by day

Live day by day.
Though the autumn leaves are withering round thy
way,
Walk in the sunshine. It is all for thee.
Push straight ahead as long as thou canst see.
Dread not the winter whither thou mayest go;
But when it comes, be thankful for the snow.
Onward and upward. Look and smile and pray—
Live day by day.

JULIA HARRIS MAY

CHAPTER EIGHT

Open the Door!

Open the door, let in the air;
The winds are sweet and the flowers are fair;
Joy is abroad in the world today,
If our door is wide, it may come this way—
    Open the door!

Open the door, let in the sun;
He hath a smile for every one;
He hath made of the raindrops gold and gems,
He may change our tears to diadems—
  Open the door!

Open the door of the soul; let in
Strong, pure thoughts which will banish sin;
They will grow and bloom with a grace divine,
And their fruit shall be sweeter than that of the vine.
  Open the door!

AUTHOR UNKNOWN

What a gloriously refreshing thought! Breathe deeply. Can't you almost feel the fresh air and sunshine, the warmth and happiness flowing through the open door of your home? To me an open door symbolizes hospitality, which is one of the world's great arts. The dictionary defines hospitality as "being disposed to entertain with generous kindness." It can hardly be defined in a better way. Even the word of God instructs us to "practice hospitality" (Romans 12:13). "Practice hospitality ungrudgingly to one another" (1 Peter 4:9). "A lover of hospitality" (Titus 1:8, K.J.V.). Open your door and invite into your home your friends, your acquaintances, those who need you.

Entertaining offers so much joy, so much satisfaction. Is there a more pleasant experience than making others happy? Hospitality is sharing with others the best *you* have. It is not "keeping up with the Joneses." One woman expressed it well when she said, "The best way to keep up with the Joneses is not to try." Put *your* time, *your* efforts, *your* ideas, and *your* heart into *your* entertaining and, with a little know-how, you will be prepared to entertain even royalty, no matter how humble your home might be.

That "little bit of know-how" is what we are going to discuss in the next few pages. Onward!

Entertaining is quite informal nowadays. Families today have smaller homes, less help, and are much more informal in their way of life. High on the popularity list are buffet suppers (no matter how small your home or apartment is, you can always serve a delightful buffet supper), informal evenings around the fireplace with your friends, novelty parties, and coffee parties.

BUFFET SUPPERS

The basic ingredient for any party is people. Get enough nice people under the same roof, and you're bound to have a successful party. When you make out your guest list, include some good conversationalists, some good listeners, and some humorists, too. ("It's easy to understand how a man can die from laughing, but not how one can live without it.") Mix up your company. Don't feel that you should have the same neighborhood group all the time. Invite some neighbors, some of your husband's business associates and their wives, and perhaps some friends from your church. You'd be surprised what an interesting evening is in store when new faces are present, and new ideas can be exchanged.

95

Telephoning an invitation is best, in my opinion. It is more personal, it gives you, as the hostess, the opportunity to explain details clearly; you will also know more definitely and more quickly which of your guests to expect. Generally speaking, invitations should be extended a week to ten days in advance. Of course, there are often exceptions to the rule. I think it's such fun to do things on the spur of the moment, too. Don't you?

Preparedness. I'm groping for the words that will emphasize strongly enough how important it is to be a prepared hostess. Mother, a pencil and a pad of paper can be your dearest friends when you're getting ready for company. A hostess *must* be well organized, or the whole party may be a failure. My pre-party schedule usually runs something like this;

Two days before party: scrub, wax, polish the house till it fairly glistens. Polish silver, press linens to be used, write party menu and grocery list carefully.

Day before:
   A.M. Shop for groceries.
   P.M. Bake, *prepare salads and everything that can possibly be prepared ahead of time.*

Party day: Set table early, put final touches on the house, fix remaining foods, etc. Allow ample time for yourself. Relax in a bubble bath, powder your face with sunshine, and be the most lovely relaxed hostess possible.

Even if it means that you must make some jet-like movements for a few days, when party time arrives take ten deep breaths and *relax*. If the hostess is not relaxed and poised and happy, she cannot expect her guests to be. When the doorbell rings, the party has begun. Let every guest know that you consider it a pleasure to entertain them in your home.

Either the host or the hostess may greet the guests at the door. Or, if you are entertaining at an early hour, and the children are still awake, appoint one of them as "butler." Dress your son up in his sharpest bow tie and shiniest face (for such an occasion he may even wash behind his ears), or dress your daughter in her fluffiest, frilliest dress and curliest locks, and send one of them to greet the guests with a smile, and have them lead the guests into the bedroom where they are to put their wraps. This will give you and your husband an opportunity to be in the living room to introduce your guests as they arrive. Children enjoy parties, if they can participate. Give them a definite duty; a child who is allowed to help will, in most cases (I guess there always will be a few sweet little rebels to throw my psychology right out the nearest window), automatically be on his best behavior.

Introductions. The first important function of the host and hostess is to be certain that each new arrival is introduced and does not feel "left out" in any way.

At a very large party the newcomers are introduced to several guests near at hand. Early in a big party, or at any kind of smaller gathering, each guest, upon arrival, is introduced to the group as a whole, "This is Liz Scott," or, "I'd like you all to meet Mr. and Mrs. Leslie Scott," or, "Liz and Les Scott." Then the host or hostess takes the Scotts around the circle to meet the other guests. Their names need not be mentioned again, unless someone may have missed the initial introduction.

Wouldn't it be terrific if we could actually revive the age of chivalry? But—sigh! I guess that those days are gone forever. But, of course, there are certain etiquette essentials that even our modern husbands must comply with. Men do arise when being introduced to a woman; the woman, however, only rises when she is being introduced to an elderly lady, or a clergyman, or a dignitary, or a very elderly gentleman.

* * * Just a little note I must insert. As a guest, be prompt; never be early; and, if you will be detained more than fifteen minutes, do phone your hostess * * *

Now, on with the buffet supper! Time for a little appetizer, something refreshing. Try one of these:

> In your prettiest glass cups place some chilled fruits, and pour on some icy ginger ale.
>
> Grape juice poured over pineapple sherbert (try various juice and sherbert combinations).
>
> An old favorite is chilled tomato juice, but season it well.

Serve your appetizers on a pretty tray with interesting little napkins and perhaps some novelty crackers topped with cheese and a slice of a pimento olive.

When the buffet is ready, simply invite your guests to stand and ask your husband—the king—to say the grace. If there is a clergyman present, of course he may ask the blessing. It is *always* proper to say grace in a Christian home, even if there are those present who are not professing Christians. Here is a meaningful testimony to the fact that this is a Christian home and that those who live in the home are grateful to God for every blessing. We never know just when a seed may bear fruit, do we?

After the blessing, the hostess asks one of the ladies to start, and the other guests to follow her. Mmmm! On to the food. The food? The food! What are we going to eat? Let's look at the lovely, tempting table. A dinner should always be a feast for the eyes as well as for the tongue. Even the contrast of colors and food textures have been considered by the smart hostess. Her table center is a delightful conversation piece; it looks lovely with her cloth and napkins; and notice how the silver and dishes sparkle? The plates, silverware, and napkins are at one extreme end of the table. No back stepping is necessary. If you are serving—perhaps a creamed specialty over parsleyed, buttered rice—of course you would put the dish of rice before the creamed dish for the convenience of your guests.

Now, what are we eating? Here are a few recipes that are economical and yet have company sparkle:

MEATS

Meat Loaf Meringue Pie

Put your favorite meat loaf into a pretty 10-inch pie plate. Bake at 350° for one hour. Swirl mashed potatoes on top of meat, top with a soft cheese spread and pop under the broiler for a few minutes. Serve in pie plate placed on a pretty platter. Slice in wedges, sprinkle with paprika. Chili sauce anyone?

Easy Beef Stroganoff

(Serve it right from the skillet)

1 pound of round steak cut in fine strips
1 medium can of mushrooms (which have been sauteed)
2/3 cup of water
1 envelope of onion soup mix

Brown meat well in skillet, season, add water and mushrooms, stir in soup mix.

Blend 1 cup dairy sour cream with 2 tablespoons of flour—add to skillet mixture. Simmer gently till sauce is thickened slightly. Serve over hot buttery noodles or rice.

POTATOES

(Try to make a spud exciting!)

Wrap your baked potatoes in foil while baking—serve them with cheese, butter, or sour cream and chives.

100

Potato Cheese Bake (my husband's favorite)

3 large potatoes
4 small onions
1 tablespoon of flour
1 teaspoon of salt. Dash of pepper.
1 teaspoon of sage
1/3 cup of cream
1/4 cup of shredded cheese—mild
5 slices of bacon

Slice potatoes and onions thin; put layer of potatoes in greased baking dish. Sprinkle with flour mixed with salt, pepper, and sage. Now a layer of onion, flour mixture, potato layer, Pour cream over the top, sprinkkle with cheese. Top with bacon slices. 1 hour at 350° (cover with foil first half hour). Serves 4-6.

Potato-Vegetable All in One Dish

Prepare 3 packages of frozen mixed vegetables according to package directions. Butter and season vegetables. Add two cans of tomato soup and put entire mixture in buttered casserole. Swirl potatoes and cheese over top of casserole and bake for 15 minutes at 350°.

VEGETABLES

Here again, let's be a little different. Any good recipe book has delicious recipes for vegetable casseroles. Corn pudding is a favorite with many. Frozen peas and onions in a cream sauce. Top buttered corn niblets with dashes of pimento. Slivered almonds atop your French green beans, or here is a good recipe for French green beans:

3 packages of frozen French style green beans
2 cans mushroom soup
½ cup of milk
salt
4 tablespoons of butter
1 package of frozen French fried onion rings

Cook green beans separately. Add soup, milk, seasoning. Top with butter and package of onion rings. 350° —1 hour.

I like to serve two vegetables when company comes— then you can be almost sure to please.

SALADS

5 Cup Salad

1 cup of orange sections
1 cup of pineapple chunks
1 cup of tiny marshmallows
1 cup of flaked coconut
1 cup of sour cream
Let stand in refrigerator over night.

A tossed salad with lots of variety in it is always tempting when served in a large salad bowl. Or, try tinting a whipped cream fruit salad pink or light green—adding a little mayonnaise—and freezing the mixture in round ice cream cartons. So nice to have ready at a minute's notice. Unmold on greens and slice in rounds.

How About a "Flaming" Jello Mold?

Select your prettiest crystal serving bowl or a fancy mold. Now, top your favorite fruit jello mold with a generous mound of whipped cream, sprinkle with broken nuts and then place cherry halves, pear halves, or peach halves on top—add a lemon extract soaked sugar lump to the center of each fruit half, and light lumps with a match. Serve immediately. Try this idea on some of your desserts too.

A crispy relish tray—do take a few extra moments to curl your carrots, slice your pickles, and arrange your olives, etc. Keep dish and all in refrigerator till serving time.

Hot rolls—unusual shapes and types of rolls. Use an interesting "bread basket."

After the main course, casually collect the dinner plates (a tea cart is such a help!) and return with piping hot coffee and a scrumptious but light refrigerator dessert that has been prepared the day before. Some people like to wait fifteen minutes or so before coffee and dessert.

103

DESSERTS

Banana Cream Delight

Cream ½ cup of butter or margarine, add 2 eggs, 1 teaspoon of vanilla and a 1 pound box of powdered sugar. Beat at medium speed of mixer till smooth—add ½ cup of chopped pecans, if desired. Spread mixture in a baked and cooled graham cracker crust (a 10 x 6 pan or 10 inch pie plate) top with sliced bananas and lastly spread ½ pint whipping cream—sweetened slightly—over top. Refrigerate several hours before serving.

Raspberry Mallow pie

This time try a coconut crust. Recipe is on coconut box.
Filling: 1 package of frozen raspberries—thawed
           16 marshmallows
           1 teaspoon of lemon juice
           1 cup of heavy cream, whipped
Drain juice from berries and add enough water to juice to make ½ cup. Heat in top of double boiler, add marshmallows and heat till they're melted. Cool, add lemon juice and chill until mixture begins to congeal. Fold in drained raspberries and whipped cream. Pour into crust and chill till firm. Garnish with whipped cream.

Lemon Meringue Dessert

Meringue; Preheat oven to 450°. Beat 5 egg whites, ¼ teaspoon of salt till foamy. Add ½ teaspoon of cream of tartar. Beat till stiff. Add 1 and ½ cups of sugar—1 tablespoon at a time. Beat at medium speed of mixer. Add 1 teaspoon of vanilla. Beat 15 minutes.

Put in buttered 9 x 9 pan. Put in oven. Turn off heat. Don't peek till morning. In the morning spread with ½ pint of cream, whipped, and lemon topping.

Lemon topping; Beat till thick 5 egg yolks—beat in ½ cup of sugar. Blend in 4 tablespoons of lemon juice and 3 tablespoons of lemon rind. Cook till thick. When cool spread on meringue and put in refrigerator for several hours before serving.

Well, I don't know about you, but I'm full just from thinking about all of these rich foods. Remember this is *company* fare. If we ate like this every day, we'd soon be twice our present size. All during the meal soft dinner music has been playing on the hi-fi or stereo, candlelight has added that necessary warmth and elegance, and the hostess has been wearing a fancy hostess apron—one that is saved for just such occasions as this.

If the children were included in this supper, they were served separately at their own "party" in the kitchen or playroom. The parents can relax and enjoy the meal, and the children actually prefer it that way. Or, perhaps the children were all fed before the adults began.

Delightful buffet supper, wasn't it? Such a relaxed and efficient hostess. Wonder how she does it?

Before we leave the subject of food altogether, let me just suggest that you really read and devour at least one good homemaking magazine monthly. Study and clip recipes, carefully observe table settings, serving suggestions, and centerpieces. Keep your recipe file orderly. Always be on the prowl for a new idea for the table.

INFORMAL EVENING GET-TOGETHER

Picture the setting with me. It's 8:30 P.M. The kiddies are all in dreamland, the fireplace is crackling, soft music is playing, candles are lighted, and the doorbell rings. Here are your guests! Such a happy group— all ready for an informal evening of good conversation, good fellowship, and good laughter. The guests are all settled, and in you come with a tempting snack tray which you have prepared in advance. Let's see, what's on it? Crackers of all kinds, chips, dips, pretzels, ham cubes, and herring pieces on colored tooth picks, olives and pickles.

Look how the faces of your guests light up! Pass

chilled glasses of pop and coasters and little napkins and sit down to enjoy your guests. As a well-organized hostess, you've even lined up in your mind a few conversation pieces to be used in case of a lag in the conversation.

After an evening of games or conversation, you'll be ready for coffee. Yes, steaming hot coffee and a man's dessert, such as a warm fruit pie ala mode, or a luscious, moist cake ala mode, or a novelty dessert such as;

Harvest Torte

Sift—2 cups of flour
   2 cups of sugar
   2 teaspoons of soda
   ½ teaspoon of salt

Add—3 beaten eggs
   1 no. 2½ can fruit cocktail
   ¾ cup of chopped dates

Put in 13 x 9 pan. Sprinkle on top;
   1 cup of brown sugar
   ¾ cup of chopped pecans

One hour and twenty minutes at 275°.

Serve warm—topped with ice cream or whipped cream.

Pass a dish of mixed nuts, too.

Remember to let yourself be entertained as well as your guests. It's not only good for you; it's essential. "All work and no play makes mother a dull girl!"

107

NOVELTY PARTIES

You must decide what kind of party you can give most gracefully with the space, money, time, and ideas you have. Whether it is a Hawaiian luau, an Oriental party, a New Year's Eve party, a surprise birthday party, a Valentine's Day celebration, a Christmas open house, an election brunch, a hard times party. Whatever your idea is—play it up to the hilt! Let your decorations, food, table, music, games, and dress all fit perfectly into the pattern. Check with your local library for party books and party ideas. Use your imagination—really let it go—and your party will be a barrel of fun for everyone.

COFFEE PARTIES

"Hello, Myrt? This is Sue. Bring the kiddies and c'mon over for a coffee party tomorrow morning about 10 A.M. I've asked Nina, Millie, June, Anna, Jean, and Sylvia too. It'll be such fun to get together again." Smart Sue has the coffee all perked when her company arrives. The children have their own get-together on a little table: juice in paper cups and oatmeal cookies will delight them. The mothers will have a chance really to enjoy each other's company this way. Have a coffee party soon. Invite several mothers in to meet your new neighbor. Vary your coffee party guest list.

Learn to open wide the doors of your home to those who need your friendship and attention. Love people, mother dear. See the good in everyone. Our heavenly Father has created each of His children with his own particular gifts, talents, and insights. He has a perfect plan for each life; He loves each of us more than we can ever imagine, and He longs to call us His own. If our Christian hospitality can be a means of showing others the beauty and joy and contentment of the Christ-centered home and life, then let us entertain joyously in the name of our Lord and Savior.

OPEN Your Doors!

Revelation 3:20:

> *"Behold, I stand at the door and knock; if any man hears my voice and opens the door, I will come in to him and will sup with him, and he with me."*

Could it be, mothers, that right now the Savior stands *outside* the door of your homes—and your hearts?

OPEN the door!

CHAPTER NINE

How Big Is Your World?

A FARMER once said that if you draw a circle of chalk on a barn floor, swing a hen around in the air and then set her down in the circle, she won't be able to cross the line. She's a prisoner in the chalk circle. Now, I have never seen this demonstrated with a hen, but I do know that it is all too true of many housewives. We are so enclosed in our own little worlds that our minds are shrinking, our curiosities are dimmed, our ideas are at a standstill, our imaginations are blank, our inspirations have ceased. We can easily become household robots, if we forget that we *must* push out the boundaries of our horizons and press on to gain a thrilling experience of life in all its fullness.

Tell me, how long has it been since you have eagerly toyed with a new idea? How many weeks, months, years has it been since your mind has cried out for a new area of life to study? A woman needs to be alert, abreast of the times. Have you ever had the experience of being out socially with a group of well-informed people and finding that you have no real knowledge of the topics they are discussing? It leaves you with rather a "how-ignorant-and-uninformed-I-am" type of feeling, doesn't it? But, when you get home again, what do you do about it? Do you forget it, or allow yourself to be challenged to greater heights?

I must confess that I hold the least amount of admiration for a person who feels, "I have arrived." If he feels as if he does not need any more knowledge, if he feels perfectly satisfied with his present state of mind and heart, I pity him!

Phillips Brooks said:

"Bad will be the day for every man when he becomes absolutely contented with the life he is living, with the thoughts that he is thinking, with the deeds he is doing, when there is not forever beating at the doors of his soul something larger which he knows that he was

111

meant and made to do because he is still, in spite of all, the child of God."

You can't stop people from thinking, they say—it's getting them started that's so difficult. We simply cannot be at our best, unless our minds are active; pray for that thirst for knowledge and wisdom.

George MacDonald wrote: "If instead of a gem or even a flower, we could place the gift of a lovely thought in the heart of a friend, that would be giving as the angels give."

Mother, how do you spend your leisure time? The way you use your leisure time may be a much greater indication of your life's goals than the way you perform your daily tasks, because the things you do in your free time are almost always the result of free choice. Life is the whole. Our loving God is interested in every part of it; we are responsible to Him for all of life— for our leisure hours as well as our working hours. Our Lord knows our thoughts; He understands our weaknesses. He has given us brains, and He expects us to use them. What our minds feed on, that is what we are going to become. What is your mind feeding on? Soap operas, low grade reading materials, gossip, glorified ideas of self? We need to feed on the *great* thoughts, the *great* ideals, and the *great* inspirations. A noble ideal, a noble thought can help to make a noble life. God help us! We are so weak, we fail so often, we are so easily influenced. We need strength of character! We need courage! We must let our minds feast on the courageous and noble things, and we shall find that our lives will be elevated to heights that we never dreamed were attainable. The moments are so few. We must use them wisely.

> *I have just a minute,*
> *Only sixty seconds in it,*
> *Forced upon me—*
> *Can't refuse it—*
> *Didn't seek it—*
> *Didn't choose it—*
> *But it's up to me to use it.*
> *I must suffer if I lose it,*
> *Give account if I abuse it,*
> *Just a tiny little minute,*
> *But eternity is in it.*

AUTHOR UNKNOWN

The areas of life that may be of interest to me, you may not find quite so interesting. But, if our minds and eyes and hearts are open, we shall see many areas of life that arouse our interest, that delight our souls, that tickle our curiosities. God has a perfect, intricate, and beautiful design for each of the trillions of snow-flakes that have fallen. Do we dare to doubt that He has a perfect and intricate and beautiful design for the life of each one of us? There is only one of each of us in this world; let us not be drawn too tightly into a mold. Be an individual thinker. What are *your* interests?

I'd like to suggest that each of you adopt a study plan. Let life be your university. Pick out some area of life that really interests *you*. Study every side of it, learn all that you can about it; when your thirst for knowledge on the subject is quenched, begin a new study on another subject. Such a rich, full, exciting world we live in: God's world! We, as God's children, should want to know as much as we possibly can about our world. "Learn as if you are going to live forever. Live as if you are going to die tomorrow."

Here are some "study" suggestions. Which of these areas are you most interested in?

Travel

It does cost a lot of money to travel. But, have you ever considered traveling via books? Take a lengthy European tour. Read about the traditions, the customs, the way of life, the history, the geography, and the resources of each of the European countries. Study them one by one. Such beautiful colored photographs and slides are available at your library that  you can look at them and almost feel you're there. When you feel that you know and understand the people of Europe, travel to South America, and then to the Orient, and on to Africa. A world tour—at no expense. And, if the day ever does arrive that you are able to take a trip to a foreign country, how much richer your experience will be because of the knowledge you have acquired through study.

Disease

Perhaps a loved one has been taken by cancer, heart disease, polio, or muscular dystrophy, or another dread disease. You are interested in finding out as much as you can about the disease. Study its history, its symtoms, its known treatment, the research being conducted. Above all else, find out what you can do to help those afflicted with a serious disease. Not just in terms of money, but by means of service, gifts, letters, volunteer work. We are our brothers' keepers! No man is an island. No man lives alone!

Albert Schweitzer says: "It's not enough merely to exist. You must do something more. Seek always to do some good somewhere. Every man has to seek in his own way to make his own self more noble and to realize his own true worth. You must give some time to your fellow man. Even if it's a little thing, do something for those who have need of help. For remember, you don't live in a world all your own, your brothers are here too."

Poetry

A poet has a gift of God in his heart and at his fingertips. Through the reading of a poem we can look into the very heart of the poet. There are poems of every variety imaginable. There are the deep and profound pieces of poetry, the light and lyrical gems,

115

the philosophical varieties, and the homespun and humorous poems, to add warmth and gaiety to our life. Collect thought jewels from the poetry you read, and store these jewels safely in the recesses of your heart and mind.

Child Psychology

I do not feel that we are truly prepared mothers. So few of our classes in school, so few of our experiences, have been geared to our preparation for the responsible role of motherhood. To a certain degree we are born to be mothers and do have natural instincts, of course. But let us be realistic! There is a great deal to be learned from those who have devoted their lives to the understanding of children and their growth mentally, physically, and spiritually. Read many of the available books on understanding children. All of the knowledge we can acquire in this area can often be applied immediately. So many behavior and discipline problems could be eliminated, if parents only knew how to cope intelligently with them. Don't you wonder at times if our little ones perhaps have their own "parent psychology"? Well then, as a "defense mechanism," we as parents should definitely make a study of the wholesome and down-to-earth approach to child psychology. Don't you agree? Child psychology is an excellent study idea for those who do not have small children, too: Sunday school teachers, grandparents, good neighbors, and people who simply like children. "Lo, sons are an heritage from the Lord, the fruit of the womb is his reward" (Psalm 127:3).

116

Flower Arranging

Are you the type of woman who enjoys working with her hands? Do you have a flair for the creative and artistic? Many excellent books and pamphlets are written on the subject of floral arrangements. Working with flowers—colorful expressions of our Father's artistry—can be very inspiring. Perhaps your service might be that of arranging flowers to give to the sick, and the shut-ins.

Politics

Many women in our time are keenly interested in politics. We must be well-informed voters. Do you stand for one party or another because your family has always done so, or have you done some *independent* thinking on the subject? Study the party platforms, the history of the parties, the records of the parties, on a national and state level. Learn to know the candidates for office and what they stand for through your reading. We can never maintain a government "of the people, by the people, and for the people" unless *we,* the people, are interested and informed on government in our great country.

Art

Can you look deeply into a beautiful painting and "lose yourself" in its message? Can you walk through an art gallery and appreciate the inspiration and feeling that originated the brush strokes? A sculptor's hands create a meaningful image to be understood. Do you understand? Would you like to? The Master, the greatest Artist, has painted and sculptured a masterpiece that can never be equalled: our world. He has sculptured the hills, the canyons, the mountains, the rivers. But His greatest work is man. And to some men He has given the gift of artistry. May we see and feel and appreciate this gift.

Education and Schools

Many schools are overcrowded, run down, and in poor condition. The increasing birth rate is making the situation even more crucial. What can *we* do in our own communities to help? Education is vital! The future of our country to a large degree lies in our educational system. Study it and work to improve America's educational standards. O, that we might realize the great significance of the molding and sustaining of each young, open mind. We must each be actively interested in our schools, in the parent-teacher associations, in building programs, and in the actions of our local school boards. We must narrow our national educational problems down to our communities and ourselves.

Music

How I love it! There is so much to learn about it, so much to appreciate. To hear the works of a great composer should make one stand in awe of such God-given talent. Music has the power to guide our emotions and feelings. Happy, gay music will put a smile on our lips; great and mighty choruses may send a chill through our bodies; a soft, lilting song will soothe and comfort us, a love song will warm our hearts, a rhythmic tune will set our foot to tapping, a great hymn will bring inspiration to our souls. Christianity has come through the ages singing God's praises.

You are not too old to play an instrument, if you sincerely desire to learn to do so. Have you ever thought of joining an evening class in music appreciation? Purchase season tickets to a concert series. Let your musical tastes guide your record selections. Include a variety of music in your collection. Learn to take a song along with you.

> *When you take the road*
> *At the dawn of day,*
> *When you lift your load*
> *And are on your way,*
> *Just to keep you glad*
> *And make you strong*
> *When the walking's bad*
> *Take a song along.*

> DOUGLAS MALLOCH
> *Youth's Favorite Poems*, III, 24

Sewing and Designing

To be perfectly honest, sewing on a button is a chore for me. I must admit, however, that one of my fondest ambitions is to learn to sew and design my own clothes. Most of us have our own ideas about what colors and styles we like best on ourselves. A talented seamstress can see her ideas take form. She can sew to please her family and friends, and save money, too. What a good feeling it must be to receive a compliment on an outfit you have made with your own hands, and perhaps even designed with your own ideas. Creativity is a treasure to be used, not stored away.

American History

Were you the high school girl who received such good grades in your history courses? You really did enjoy studying our nation's history, didn't you? Have you opened a history book since high school or college to reread the pages on Columbus, the thirteen colonies, Valley Forge, the Declaration of Independence, the Lewis and Clark expedition, the westward move, the gold rushes and Indian wars, our great presidents, congresses, the World Wars? We have a rich American heritage. "America! America! God shed His grace on thee." Americans! Fall on your knees in thankfulness. Ours is the land of the free.

"Our father's God, to thee,
Author of liberty,
To thee we sing;
Long may our land be bright
With freedom's holy light;
Protect us by thy might,
Great God, our King."

If you love your country, learn about your country. Be *proud* Americans. Thank God for the privilege of being a part of these United States of America, "one nation, under God, indivisible, with liberty and justice for all." Never take this privilege for granted.

Writing

What a thrill it is to put your thoughts down in black and white. Millions of words that could never be spoken can be written. Courage can be found in the pen. If someone would have told me when I was so eagerly writing for the high school weekly that some-day I'd write books, I would have laughed. But here

I am just writing to you the things that are overflowing from my heart. A person must write from his own experience. Now when new ideas are kindled in my mind, I feel restless until I write them down in black and white, and put them in the file. Do you enjoy writing? Then, don't be afraid to tackle pencil and paper; put your heart and prayers into what you write, and don't give up.

Youth Work

Our young people want to enjoy life and adventure. Young people are vibrant! They want life in technicolor, and we, as adults, must show them by our lives that in Christ we find happiness, power, joy, and adventure. Our Lord said He came that we might have abundant life. Every thrill of a lifetime is to be found by the courageous young men and young women who have the courage to live for God. Christ offered the greatest challenge when He spoke two words, "Follow me."

Are you concerned about the young people who are headed in the wrong direction? Then don't just sit there and read stories of teen-age violence and say, "Tch, tch!" Do something about it. Study delinquency problems and causes. If you are sincerely interested in troubled teen-agers and have the time, consider some phase of voluntary youth work. Consult your pastor or local youth commission for advice and information. Act now.

Bible Study

Of course, every **Christian** should be—must be—studying the Bible. But some of us would like to become real Bible students. Perhaps we have not had the Bible training in our background that we would like to have had; perhaps our faith is new, and we are like newborn babes, sincerely desiring spiritual food. Where to start? Here are a few suggestions:

- The new translations of the Bible help to make the Word more understandable. We can read the great truths written in our modern-day language.
- Attend an adult Bible class on Sunday mornings.
- Does your church have a mid-week Bible study? If so, attend regularly.
- Since we are not all gifted theologians, consider this: Read from cover to cover an older child's recommended Bible story book.
- Many Bible schools offer Bible correspondence courses. Inquire.
- Read the Bible daily. Pray before you read, as you read, and when you have finished reading. God will give you understanding, if you but ask.

Mission Work

How much do you actually know about the home and foreign missionary efforts of your church? Where are the mission fields? What progress is being made? What are the conditions? What are the particular needs of the mission fields?

Your missionaries need your prayers, your financial help, your letters, your gifts, and your interest. God has called these men and these women to serve Him in the mission fields. Remember that *we are all colaborers.* "Go into all the world and preach the gospel to the whole creation." That means you and me, as well as those who have crossed the seas in the name of our Lord. God bless them! And God help us to help them!

Nature

In this day and age of cars and houses and buildings and people and places and things and gadgets, are we losing the thrill of simple communion with God through nature? Do we know the soul-satisfying experience of walking, alone, down a country lane, engulfed in the beauty of a crisp fall afternoon, or the inspiration that comes from breathing deeply the fresh and fragrant air of a spring evening, or the magic touch of the invigorating, wintry winds as they brush across our faces leaving a glowing pink "love pat" on our

cheeks? To be alone, out of doors, away from traffic, people, and civilization, what a wonderful experience it is! Our heavenly Father loves to speak to us through nature. Are we listening?

VOICES FROM GOD

I love to hear the patter of the rain,
It gives my heart a thrill;
Each drop a message seems to me from God:
"Children, I love you still."

Into the deeper woodland for retreat
I wandered, sad and lonely all the while,
Until I plucked a flower at my feet,
And, looking into it, beheld God smile.

Faith flourishes in solitude.

God speaks through silent things:
The vastness of a midnight's inky sky;
The awesome splendor of a day's grey dawning;
The warmness of a high-noon's glowing sun;
The grandeur of a twilight hour;
The freshness of the earth's awakening;
The peacefulness of its sleeptime . . .

125

God speaks through silent things;
  The hush of meditation's moments;
  The solemness of prayer-bent heads;
  The strength of a soul to heaven's music set;
  The radiance of hope's sure flame;
The might of faith's assurance;
  The majesty of love's steadfastness . . .

Through silent things like these He says,
"Be still, and know that I am God."

T. M. WERSELL

There is so much to learn; this list of areas of life to study could go on endlessly: great women of the world, church history, racial prejudice, social problems, ceramics, foreign foods—and on and on and on. But now it's up to you, dear mother; this is your world, too. Learn all that you possibly can about it.

You don't have time to study? Funny, isn't it, how we can always find time to do the things we really want to do. Tuck the children tenderly in bed at night, your working day is over. Use your free evenings to relax and read—the newspaper, the finest magazines, your church publications, and books.

Thank God for books that take us to
The mountaintops, where we may view
The wondrous panorama there
Of earth and sky and sea and air;
The fleecy clouds that dot the sky;
The lonely eagle soaring high;
The rainbow's varicolored hues;
The flowers wet with fragrant dews;
The merchant ships that sail the seas;
The aspen rustling in the breeze;
The farmer raking new-mown hay;

127

The bright-eyed children at their play;
The shepherd watching o'er his sheep;
The weary toiler, seeking sleep;
The friends, once parted, reconciled;
The mother crooning to her child.

Thank God for books in which to find
All that is noble, true, and kind,
That show the path good men have trod
And found their way through Christ to God.

AUTHOR UNKNOWN
Youth's Favorite Poems, II, 29

Develop your minds, elevate your thoughts, broaden your world; but always remember the words of Daniel Webster,

The greatest thought I ever had was that of my individual responsibility to God.

CHAPTER TEN

Your God and You

OUR GOD is real! Why is it that millions of people in our so-called Christian nation have the idea that our God, the King of kings, the Lord of heaven and earth, is way out in "left field" someplace, that He doesn't quite know what's going on in this world? They believe He's there in case of an emergency—sickness, sorrow, or death—but that is His only place in their lives. Only through our lives, and the lives of all those who truly know Him, can we show the world that *our God is real,* that He is walking beside us each step of the way. And when we fall and fail Him miserably, as so often we do, He's right there by our side to pick us up again and lead us on. He's there by our side every moment of every hour of every day, whispering to us, "Let me bear your worries, burdens, and troubles; let me be your strength." Then very softly He whispers, "I love you." Think of it! He knows us, our thoughts, our motives, our desires; and yet He loves us more than we can ever realize.

People outside the church judge the church not by the buildings erected for worship, not by bits of sermons they read in newspaper accounts, not even by the Bible, but by you and me and all who profess His holy name. What kind of ambassadors of the heavenly King are we? Let your light shine; the souls of men are in the balance.

Arise, shine, for your light has come, and the glory of the Lord has risen upon you (Isaiah 60:1).

A long-faced, unlovely type of Christian character is not true holiness. It is merely the skeleton without the covering flesh. Jesus Christ was not only pure and virtuous, strong and powerful, but He was also full of the warm attractiveness of love.

Christianity is not weak! It is the greatest power the world has ever known! When the Christian faith takes hold of a person, it turns him into an alert and responsive human being, one who knows the power of the Holy Spirit in his daily life. Christ's transforming power can be applied with startling success to our everyday problems. Our God will meet every need.

You and I: "But, dear God, why do we have so many trials and troubles? We cannot bear them."

God's Word says: "Count it all joy, my brethren, when you meet various trials, for you know that the testing of your faith produces steadfastness" (James 1:2-3). "God is . . . a very present help in trouble" (Psalm 46:1).

You and I: "There are so many things that we really need."

God's Word says: "Those who seek the Lord lack no good thing" (Psalm 34:10). "And God is able to provide you with every blessing in abundance, so that you may always have enough of everything and may provide in abundance for every good work" (2 Corinthians 9:8). "My God will supply every need of yours according to his riches in glory in Jesus Christ" (Philippians 4:19).

You and I: "Dear Lord, we get so tired. We are physically and mentally exhausted by the end of the day."

God's Word says: "Come to me, all who labor and are heavy-laden, and I will give you rest" (Matthew 11:28).

131

You and I: "There are times when we feel so alone. Loneliness is hard to bear."

God's Word says: "I am with you always, to the close of the age" (Matthew 28:30).
"I will never fail you nor forsake you" (Hebrews 13:5).

You and I: "Nobody really understands us! Our efforts and our words are often misunderstood."

God's Word says: "The Lord is the everlasting God, . . . his understanding is unsearchable" (Isaiah 40:28).

You and I: "Oh, to find real, lasting peace in our lives!"

God's Word says: "The peace of God, which passes all understanding, will keep your hearts and your minds in Christ Jesus" (Philippians 4:7).

You and I: "Our fears weigh us down, dear Savior."

God's Word says: "Let not your hearts be troubled, neither let them be afraid" (John 14:27).

You and I: "There is so much work to be done, and we just haven't the strength to do it all."

God's Word says: "He gives power to the faint, and to him who has no might he increases strength" (Isaiah 40:29).

You and I: "We want so to have real victory in our lives."

God's Word says: "But thanks be to God, who gives us the victory through our Lord Jesus Christ" (1 Corinthians 15:57).

You and I: "Forgive us, dear Father, we think of ourselves too much."

God's Word says: "He who humbles himself will be exalted" (Luke 14:11).

You and I: "We are so sinful; we fail so often; our sins are always before us."

God's Word says: "Though your sins are like scarlet, they shall be as snow" (Isaiah 1:18).

"If we confess our sins, he is faithful and just, and will forgive us our sins and cleanse us from all unrighteousness" (1 John 1:9).

You and I: "Does He really listen when we pray?"

God's Word says: "The Lord is near to all who call upon him, to all who call upon him in truth" (Psalm 145:18).

You and I: "Dear Lord, if we are honest, we must admit that we are just not satisfied with what we have in life."

God's Word says: "For I have learned, in whatever state I am, to be content" (Philippians 4:11).

You and I: "Father, how can we "reach" You?

Jesus said: "I am the way, and the truth, and the life; no one comes to the Father, but by me" (John 14:6).

"For there is no other name under heaven given among men by which we must be saved" (Acts 4:12).

"You shall call his name Jesus, for he will save his people from their sins" (Matthew 1:21).

We are all sinners in need of a Savior; and we have a Savior, Christ the Lord. We cannot live without Him,

133

we dare not die without Him. The only way to live life victoriously is to live in faith, not any kind of faith, but faith in Jesus Christ.

We do not look at an elevator and say, "I believe that this elevator could take me to the tenth floor"; but rather, we step into that elevator! It is not enough to say, "I believe in God." If you do believe, you will put your trust and faith in Him; you will give Him your life to use for His blessed Name's sake.

Mother, wife, what is your relationship to God? *You* are the only one who can answer that question. "Every knee shall bow . . ." Everyone of us shall see Him face to face some day. We shall stand alone before our Maker. Will we hang our heads in shame, or will we be able to look up into the compassionate eyes of our Savior, and hear Him say, "Well done, good and faithful servant; inherit the place I have reserved for you, my daughter"?

GOD'S HAND

Think of stepping on shore—
And finding it Heaven!

And taking hold of a hand—
And finding it God's hand!

Of breathing a new air—
And finding it Celestial air!

Of feeling invigoration—
And finding it Immortality!

134

Of passing from storm and tempest—
To perfect Calm!

Of waking and knowing—
"I am at Home!"

Youth's Favorite Poems, I, 11

Prepare to meet your God. Life for you will never be complete and rich and beautiful without the Savior Jesus Christ.

God bless you, dear mothers! Live *beautifully* for your great God, He who is called "Wonderful Counselor, Mighty God, Everlasting Father, Prince of Peace."

Dear Father, grant unto us true family love,
That we may belong more entirely to those
  whom Thou hast given us,
Understanding each other, day by day, more
  instinctively,
Forbearing each other, day by day, more
  patiently,
Growing, day by day, more closely into oneness
  with each other and with Thee.

"As for me and my house, we will serve the Lord"
(Joshua 24:15).